—HOW TO—
GROWTH HACK
YOUR STARTUP

• CREATIVE TRACTION METHODOLOGY •

Tommaso Di Bartolo

How to GROWTH HACK your startup.
Copyright © 2019 by Tommaso Di Bartolo. All rights reserved.

Crafted with ♥ in Silicon Valley.

www.Creative-Traction.com

This book may be purchased at special discounts in bulk for promotional, educational, or business use. Please contact http://www.tommasodibartolo.com/ or send an email to be.WhatItTakes@gmail.com

Amazon: ISBN Printed in the United States of America.

Book and Jacket design by Bonach Communication
Illustrations by Fred Goldstein

10 9 8 7 6 5 4 3 2 1

First Edition

Follow The Author

(f) @DiBartoloTommaso

(in) /in/tommasodibartolo/

 @TommasoDiBartolo

(🐦) @ToDiBa

(e) www.TommasoDiBartolo.com

09 | FOREWORD BY KEN SINGER

11 | PREFACE

17 | AN INTRODUCTION - TO GROWTH HACKING

    21 | 1 - MY STORY
    25 | 2 - WHAT IS GROWTH HACKING
    31 | 3 - WHEN TO APPLY GROWTH HACKING
    38 | 4 - HOW TO APPLY GROWTH HACKING
    43 | 5 - WHO IS IT FOR

53 | PILLAR ONE:
CONVEYING PRODUCT VALUE: THE NUANCES OF COMMUNICATION

    55 | 1 - THE NUANCES OF COMMUNICATION
    60 | 2 - THE RAPID ASSESSMENT EXERCISE: HOW ARE YOU DIFFERENT
    66 | 3 - TRIGGER BASED MARKETING

73 | PILLAR TWO:
RECALIBRATE YOUR MINDSET: THE PROMOTIONAL STRATEGIES THAT LEAD TO CRAVING FANS

    75 | 1 - START BEFORE YOU START
    84 | 2 - DISCOVER THE UNCLUTTERED CHANNEL
    92 | 3 - GIVE BEFORE YOU ASK
    106 | 4 - CONTROLLED PROCRASTINATION
    109 | 5 - FEAR OF MISSING OUT
    111 | 6 - PRESENTING VALUE + STEPPING AWAY
    114 | 7 - PROACTIVE MEETING COORDINATION
    117 | 8 - MEETING TO MEETING TO WIN

123 | PILLAR THREE:
EXECUTING COHERENTLY: DISCOVER THE RIGHT TOOLS

    125 | 1 - STOP SPRAYING + PRAYING
    128 | 2 - THE G-AARRR FUNNEL: ONE STAGE AT A TIME
    149 | 3 - BUILD AN EXPERIENCE

153 | CONCLUSION: IMPLEMENTATION

157 | BONUS: HACKS

165 | GLOSSARY OF TERMS + INDEX

173 | AUTHOR BIO

ACKNOWLEDGEMENTS

First off, I want to thank God. Through God, I learned to run blind at full speed towards what I wanted, while keeping the faith in what I couldn't see.

Second, to my wife, who has forever been the one to believe and invest in our future. To she who has so often believed in me, more than I could in myself. Without her, there's absolutely no way I would be where I am today, and be blessed enough to have the family we've worked so hard to build.

To my kids, who taught me how to be a father. Who taught me true unconditional love. Who taught me that any business done is temporary, where the true legacy lies in the familial bonds we strengthen each day.

To my sister, who beyond being family has also become my best friend. To she who is always there to listen, offer advice, and be actively hands on. I am honored by our bond.

And finally, to my parents. To my mother, whom I admire so deeply; a woman of pure humbleness and persistence. And to my entrepreneurial father, to whom I am the 2.0 version. A man of great character, values and strength. A man who taught his son never to fear, always to execute, and to fight through any and all pain!

Thank you.

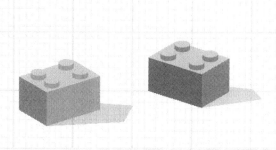

> *Never forget where you come from;*
> *it keeps you humble.*
> *But, where you come from*
> *cannot limit where you want to go!*
>
> Tommaso Di Bartolo

FOREWORD BY KEN SINGER

At Berkeley, the word "hacking" means many things. Our campus was one of the birthplaces of modern Computer Science, so it's only natural to think "computer hacking" when the term emerges in conversation. But Berkeley is also one of the engines of the Silicon Valley, where hundreds of fledgling startups blossom every year. In this community, the word "hacking" is used affectionately to mean "finding a clever solution that is cheaper or faster than the traditional path." Students pride themselves in hacking pretty much *everything*—getting into crowded classes, graduating early, landing an impossible internship, even starting a company in the basement of their fraternity house for free. "Hacking" is a way of life and in today's business climate, "growth hacking" offers a crucial competitive advantage.

However, for many startups, "growth hacking" is the only option—they simply don't have the resources to afford traditional methods. Startups lack the time or the money to launch expensive new products the "right way." They cannot afford the multi-million dollar product development cycles of IBM or the endless marketing budgets of Apple. But somehow, companies like AirBnB, WhatsApp and Twitter, often starting with just beer money, find a way to compete and eventually dominate their markets. Each of these companies has a colorful origin story full of near-death moments, market dead-ends and finally successful rebirths. The common thread that binds them? They all used clever marketing hacks to find their markets and gain initial traction.

Which brings us to this book, *How to Growth Hack your Startup*, a must read for those aspiring to gain a foothold in this impossibly competitive startup world. It explains when and how to growth hack, offers tools and techniques, and provides a roadmap for both entrepreneurs and corporate intrapreneurs. Indeed, this book provides something for everyone. For technology marketers, this book provides time tested techniques that can be implemented immediately. If you need a growth hack, just flip through the examples Tommaso shares in each chapter. For product managers and engineers, who see "marketing" as sorcery and witchcraft, these next few chapters give you critical insight into the marketing discipline—why it is so difficult and costly. For entrepreneurs, reading these pages may be the difference between your company barely surviving and happily thriving.

Ultimately, the goal of "marketing" in a startup is to find early adopters, understand why they were attracted to your solution and leverage that knowledge to access a wider audience. In a way, "Marketing" is Hacking—not computers, but customer demand.

Today, it is not enough to simply hack the early adopter; winning companies must hack the entire market—in the parlance of the Valley, companies must be "growth hacking" at all times. However, Growth Hacking is as much an art as a science. And as with all things artistic, growth hacking requires developing customized tactics and instituting cutting edge practices to achieve success. In this book, you will acquire what is necessary to develop your own set of techniques that if practiced with discipline and attention, will give your company a competitive edge. Rest assured your competitors are growth hacking—those who master the right techniques for their business will win. Those who simply rely on the traditional marketing strategies of formulaic business schools will find themselves hacked out of the game.

—Ken Singer, Managing Director SCET I UC Berkeley

PREFACE

II don't believe in the phrase, "Teach a man how to fish, and you feed him for a lifetime."

People who primarily like to teach things are often hands off. A Startup Life, however, is all about being hands on… it's all about getting to KPI's on a daily basis. [Key Performance Indicators—tools and actions used to measure and monitor an organization's goal-oriented progress.]

I believe in training on the job.

"Watch how I fish… and when you are ready, let's fish together."

This makes one real. Puristic. Accessible. Authentic. No bullshit. Straight to the point. Driven. And above all, this moves one closer to providing real, tangible value.

Much more my style.

I care about sharing my real-life lessons learned… from an entrepreneur, for entrepreneurs. And the more entrepreneurs who absorb and apply the framework I describe in this book, as well as teach through my blog and keynotes, the more I can contribute towards reducing the scary conversion rate that **nine out of ten startups fail because they lack traction**.

And therefore supercharge more entrepreneurs to succeed.

I am currently a Silicon Valley-based entrepreneur-turned-investor focused on helping corporations to innovate, and startups to get traction.

Growth Hacking has risen to the top within the world of traction, becoming realized as the most agile way of leveraging sales and marketing.

Utilizing my three-pillar approach to growth hacking, founded upon the ideals of communication, strategy, and tools, you can—and will—increase your conversion rates, swimming confidently to the shores of traction, and out of the rough waters of weak GTM's and lost MVP's.

This process leads you to change your behaviour and business attitude, meaning that it shifts your mindset, and along with it, your understanding of Go-To-Market Strategies [GTM's]. Most importantly, this shift then allows you to unlock your **inner creativity** in clear, concise ways that motivate your buyer persona to engage naturally with your product.

> *Creative Traction Methodology provides a framework for startups that helps founders growth hack their path towards traction.*

At the end of the day, what I want to share is how I've been doing it, why it's worked, and why it will work for you.

Let me start by sharing what qualifies me to be here:

As an entrepreneur, I've had to fulfill many roles. I had to learn to grow into each and every position of any startup that needed to be fulfilled at that time. I mean, you have to, right?

You so often have to go it alone, performing tasks and jobs in ragged ways. Fighting to find the agility, find the tools, find the communication, find the strategy… and most of all, find your ability to go it alone and not be overwhelmed in the process.

Depending on which phase your startup is in, you go full speed ahead towards fulfilling whatever the company requires the most:

You are a Chief Product Officer to start out with. You are head of HR to build the A-Team and to keep it hooked. You are the interim CTO when required. You are always the Strategy Officer to guide the direction and enchant investors. You are Business Developer, to listen to what customers want and bring it back to Engineering. You are Marketing to craft value propositions that drive engagement. You are Finance—to keep the lights on, and track customer success to supercharge existing customers.

By fulfilling every job yourself, you quickly discover what you do well, and what you love to do. You unearth your talents at rapid speed, while weeding out the stuff you hate, and would much rather avoid.

And while, sure, I'm capable of running teams and breaking down the sprints; capable of doing finances, exiting the company, and running the marketing, the gift that I've found I possess—my diamond uncovered in the rough—is communication: enchanting others about what I'm working on.

What I've realized about communication is that the talent is found in how you hook the interest of the other. This includes every single person you work with; whether that be an investor, colleague, teammate, or whatever. Enchanting others about what you do—communication—is *everything*.

The structure I introduce you to in this book allows you to perform the strategy it would take five people running traditional sales and marketing methods to do, working the old school way. The structure I expand upon, in this book, is what I've built my career on.

Over the course of the last eighteen years I've built four startups, and had two exits. Three of these startups were enterprise companies, one was in consumer business. As such, I bring experience and expertise from both sides. I've been involved in almost every aspect of startups, start to finish, whether that finish ends up in success or failure.

My most recent endeavor is called Awesm Ventures. An early stage investment firm focused on startups solving a problem within the mobility industry. We are especially intrigued with data-driven startups that build next-gen experiences for the automotive, aviation, maritime, railway, oil and energy industries.

Unlike other VCs that first and foremost have a spray-and-pray approach to see what sticks, we collaborate primarily with global corporations in the mobility industry to understand their business unit challenges, and innovation goals.

We believe that everything and everybody is a product, and thus, that the market doesn't need another "traditional" VC, but a business partner for entrepreneurs and executives that understands both languages.

Instead of only listening to pitches and visions, we have a tangible understanding of what industry problems need to be solved—inside out—from the corporation's perspective.

In other words, we at **Awesm Ventures** collaborate with global mobility corporations, to help drive external innovation for them. We define external innovation as the touchpoint between the corporation and startup. We plug into their innovation department, and become the extended team—based in Silicon Valley—that helps them drive qualified interaction with startups.

Startups love it, because we go the extra mile for the startup towards the corporation. Once we see a match, we guide both parties towards POCs [Proof of Concepts]. Call Awesm Ventures a next-gen value added niche VC that creates a win-win-win situation.

A Win for the corporation seeking tangible innovation. A Win for the startup wanting to access multinationals, and a Win for our fund and our LPs, by mitigating investment risks.

Basically, we hook the fish for you, while you watch and learn *how* we do it. That's what makes us at Awesm Ventures different. And it's also what makes this process; my process unique.

I want, for you, by the end of this book, to have the confidence to run growth hacks with ease for your venture. Through my three-step approach, and the real-life examples I share with you, from my journey to yours, you will witness how I growth hack, so that you can apply the process to your startup.

I want you to know what steps you're going to take to gain traction in your startup, and be able to make business-altering changes, today.

AN INTRODUCTION

TO GROWTH HACKING

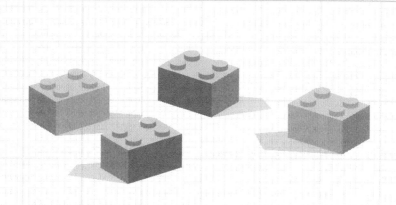

"Nine Out of Ten Startups Fail Because They Lack Traction: The Ability to Bring a Product to Market."

Why should you care about growth hacking?

Because it redefines how to bring innovation to market—much faster, and more creatively.

Growth Hacking supports startups, from transforming their business through repeatable processes using market leader Sales/Marketing tools, to a dynamic activity requiring a contemporary mindset, tools and creativity.

In the age where getting an MVP on the market doesn't necessarily require a senior developer, markets are flooded with clouds and apps that struggle to win a critical mass to make a living. As a consequence, **nine out of ten startups fail because they lack traction: the ability to bring a product to market.**

It's challenging to build a team, craft and design a product, craft the correct value proposition, raise funding… **all** of these things are difficult.

And yet, *why* do **nine out of ten** startups fail?

Because they lack traction.

Successful GTM's lead to real results—KPI's, numbers, success…. If people desire, and are using and craving your product, **this is traction**.

Traction is desire; traction is creating craving fans.

This book includes my three-step approach for how to gain traction, or as I like to say, *how to growth hack the shit out of your startup.*

And what's at the center of this three-step process of gaining traction?

Creativity.

When the shit hits the fan, human creativity starts flourishing without considering boundaries, as the fear to fail does two things:

a) ignites the power to fight for survival ["fight or flight"]

b) eliminates completely the fear of being blamed

I will tell you that moving out of your comfort zone (to reference the quote that opens this book) is the ultimate first step in growth hacking. It is vital in gaining traction—and really applies to basically every area of your life, whether business or personal.

It is challenging to find the best pathway for how to make a product successful, and my intent is to make it easier for you.

Now, having said that, there are *no* silver bullets. While I'm writing and publishing this book, there could be so many new activities that others and myself have already run. What you're reading may already be old news, to a point. The goal of the contemporary mindset is always to be at the fore of thinking ahead; always using new tools. However, the core data shared in this book *is* a mindset. The mindset is what continues to persevere through the changing times and emerging tools.

And luckily, as well, at then end of this book (in Bonus Hacks) I have included a chapter which links to a live database of contemporary hacks.

The purpose of this process; my approach to the science of growth hacking, is to empower you to think and execute uniquely, and to empower you to gain early traction, in order to avoid contributing to the statistic of *becoming one of* **the nine**.

So, ready or not, let's take that step outside your comfort zone. Grab your fishin' pole, and get started on your Go-To-Market strategy now.

1 - MY STORY

Here is a picture of my *most favorite startup* ever. My family.

On the left, there, is the CEO of our startup, my *gata*: my wife Zenaidy (who goes by Jeannie). My wife is my first and best believer, and responsible for where I am in *every* startup I've taken on.

Second from the left is our CPO, Samuel, 13 years old. He is an artist, super creative, sings and plays three instruments.

Second from the right is our Data Scientist, my eldest, David. At 17, he is a walking Wikipedia—super smart, inventive and aware.

Now, I'm the investor in this venture, though of course I am still waiting on my ROI [Return on Investment]. Still, it is by far the most exciting startup I've taken part in; the one I am most proud of.

If you think a startup is challenging, and that family is challenging... imagine doing both at the same time! A challenge, but so rewarding. And so enlightening to the ways of the world.

I was born and raised in Sicily, Italy; what people tend to call either "South Europe" or "Northern Africa". It isn't necessarily a centralized place, and definitely isn't a place well-known for business success stories.

In fact, I had two options for work when I lived there. I could either: a) be unemployed, or b) work for those not so well-known for driving legal business... aka *La Mafia*. I'm kidding (yet am serious all the same).

So, I moved to Germany, both for work and to support myself through college. I remained in Germany—after graduating with a degree in marketing from the BAW School Munich—long enough to meet my wife, who had come from Brazil to study in Germany as well.

Since I only speak Italian in my home, and my wife only speaks Portuguese; and as our kids were raised first in Germany, and now the US, they are both quad-lingual. Confusing, right... but we are so proud of the versatility of their upbringing.

I started doing business and startups around the year 2000. Fast forward, and 19 years of entrepreneurship later, I have four of those under my belt. I've had startups I grew organically [meaning without raising funds], had startups in which I raised funds, had startups wherein I had exits (two of them), had startups which failed... and founded every single startup from scratch.

All the while, I was always attracted to the vibe and location of Silicon Valley. In 2010, I followed that attraction, and started travelling back and forth between Germany and Silicon Valley quite often.

My first trip out, my goal was to: get to Silicon Valley, get a glimpse of what's really going on, and take it from there. I'd come to understand the market.

What ended up happening was—on my second day—I found myself settled into a cafe table at the Ghirardelli Chocolate Factory in San Francisco, dialing my wife. Here's how the following conversation between us went:

"How's it going out there, Tommaso?" My wife said sweetly to me.

I said to her, "Oh, well, *Gata* ["gata" means beauty in portuguese], I have to tell you two things."

"What's going on?" She asked as I readied my response,

"Well, the first thing is that I incorporated...."

"....what does that mean?"

I said, "Well, you know, I founded my first company here."

She said "Why did you found a company... if you are there just to understand things?"

"Oh, well, I... understood enough. And found that if I combine my type of personality with the vibes I feel here in Silicon Valley, we are going to do really well."

And then—smart as my wife is, and knowing how crazy I am—she said to me, "Well, you know, just come back to your family; your kids are *here* waiting for you...."

Back then, in Germany, I had roughly 30+ employees. I lived in a "nice" comfort zone.

I responded to my wife, saying, "Well, I also have to tell you the second thing."

She replied, more flatly now, "What. *What* do you mean the second thing?"

And I said, "Oh, well, I already booked another flight from Germany to Silicon Valley in three weeks."

The reason why I did that was to **push myself out of my comfort zone**.

I'm that type of a person who tries to realize their comfort zones in order to move out of them. I knew that in order to have a global impact, I had to come to Silicon Valley. And that's how I made the step into Silicon Valley. The step that took me to where I am today.

==Are you pushing yourself out of your comfort zone? What holds you back? Your country, your family, your job, your financial situation—or YOUR excuse? The excuse driven by fear, that limits you to take that step towards the unknown.==

Stop wasting your time admiring things others do. Start executing towards something you would like to change. And remember, as long as you have "only" an idea—you'll be in massive competition. Millions of others have the same chat day in and day out: "I have an idea where, if it would work, it would change the world."

You know what I'm referring to, right?

The moment in which you talk with your friends, your partner, or your family, and expand upon the idea—but as a matter of fact—it has a low impact. Why? Because it's raw, raw, raw…!

Instead, start rolling out that idea, and start solving one challenge at a time towards your goal. In that step—yes—you'll have less competition.

Good news: the smarter, faster, and better you execute, the closer you get to making an impact. And by the way, stop thinking out loud, "if I could be in Silicon Valley, things could be different!" Well, if you believe that, you know you're only a flight away. Make the move, and start experiencing it.

Take massive action today, and apply the methods, tools and tactics that hack your growth; that hack your status quo!

2 – WHAT IS GROWTH HACKING

So, what really is Growth Hacking?

Growth Hacking is the art of taking innovation to market by leveraging new tools and creative tactics, which help innovators to do more—with less, in a short period of time—and therefore helps a hustler, a hacker and a hipster in a garage to be perceived as an army.

It is the most agile way to run sales and marketing in 2020, to increase the odds of your buyer persona to engage with your product.

Unlike traditional sales and marketing plans taught in school which guide one to map out six to twelve months of project plans; where the marketing mix defines several activities ahead of time to be rolled out in consideration of the famous 4-Ps of marketing (Product, Price, Promotion and Place), with Growth Hacking it is all about plumbing tools together that your buyer persona has potentially never interacted with, which in combination with a creative way of packaging and phrasing your product offering, incentivizes and motivates your persona to take action **now**.

And by so doing, growth hacking helps to reduce the cycle from awareness to win, creating an accelerated, more engaging—and ideally, automated—repeatable process. Growth Hacking unlocks the urge and reason your persona to act now and here!

Those of us who have studied marketing in university (as I did) may have to throw all that bureaucracy that was taught right out the window. I'm not saying that the four P's of marketing are by any means obsolete. They are fundamentally right, only you may as well use a lighter, faster, KPI-optimized approach, by leveraging growth hacking.

You want that agility. To get more done, with less budget and more speed.

Once you get a taste for Growth Hacking, it changes your mindset. It changes the way you think about "leads". Due to the fact that running growth hacks puts activities on steroids, you don't fear losing a prospect, or messing up a campaign. Therefore you become more confident, as you know you have more **unique** campaigns in your pipeline you are yet to run. The thrill of seeking out and finding the appropriate hacks to accelerate your growth exponentially becomes addicting.

Growth hacking helps you to build more trust and desirability around your product, and all in the name of understanding more clearly what your persona wants from your product. Typical pitfalls on the other side include merely offering the product at a specific price, leaving it to your prospect to decide a) when to take it, b) how to access it, c) whether to go for it.

It should instead be a sort of cycle, wherein you continue to improve and implement the precise touchpoints that gain more and more conversions for your product or startup, and thus, engage your persona more directly.

Stop copying what others are doing—but **start** putting the same creative approach when building a product into your go-to-market. Expect it to be valuable and fun for the way your persona interacts with your brand.

By leveraging growth hacking activities, the touchpoints with your persona—via web, ads, video, email, bots, polls, etc.—will be different. They will be unique. You will become capable of guiding your prospects' desires and influencing the psychology of their buying decision.

Who can get your product?

- With that you define:
    - » The Role
    - » The Title
    - » The department
    - » The business unit
    - » The city
    - » The region
    - » The country

...of your persona as a form of "exclusivity" for them. By doing that the message conveys "context" and "focus" which ultimately is the fundament for knowledge. And if we are capable of conveying knowledge we build trust

How many can use it?

Instead of offering your innovation (especially early on—but not only) to "everybody", learn the skill to limit its availability:

- The first 100 receive something additional
- For 10 frequent users we provide dedicated support
- The offering is by **invitation only**
- Early adopters have a special treat for lifetime

Come from a perspective of abundance and not scarcity. Rather then thinking "price" think value, and ask yourself what your persona would respond if you ask, "How much service do you want?"
Leverage that!

For how long is the offer available?

Develop the capability to define strategic promotions (which we will discuss under PILLAR II) that make your product only available for a designated period of time:

For the length of a version type: *Salesforce*, for instance, had a "logo" and "tagline" early on for every new release they had, which they applied to run a scarcity campaign against it

- For a specific "theme" that has a start and end date, which brings new features
- For a season: Summer Edition. Winter Version....
- For a period of time... to be decided within three hours. Follow appsumo.com to get a sense for specific offer strategies they have built their business upon
- Or to be the first to get the offering—unlike the others who will have to wait longer

This will unlock the urge to act now.

You will surprise your persona as you start using tools they enjoy using, as you say things they start to become more curious about, and as you access them in ways they wouldn't ordinarily expect. This is how you will increase your conversion rates.

This, by the way, is the goal of growth hacks.

However, what I've learned—and the hard way—is that growth hacking is **not just about the tools.** They are prevalent, but they are not everything.

People often ask me for growth hacking advice, wherein I notice they are really just looking for my curated list of 400+ tools to work with, and that's it.

However, I carry no such thing, and condone no such approach.

There are *fundamental* things you have to do to prepare, before you start growth hacking, in order to do so successfully.

Reducing Growth hacking to just "tools", is like driving a race car without any training. What sounds like a great trip, may turn deadly if you've never driven a race car before, as the probability of your crashing it is very high. Much higher than, say, if you know how to run and handle the machine before starting its engine.

Allow me to translate: if you use tools without using the right tactics—aka, frequency of activity, intervals of campaign, variations of design, promotional offerings, and copies—you may very well crash your expectations, which will demotivate you and create fear. And fear is the biggest enemy of any entrepreneur as it limits your ability to act and execute towards something *others may not believe in—but we do.*

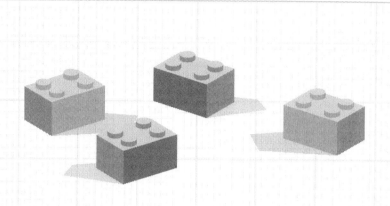

"Growth Hacking is the Agile Way to Run Sales & Marketing, To Increase the Odds of your Buyer Persona to Engage."

3 - WHEN TO APPLY GROWTH HACKING

The term Growth Hacking might itself imply—because of the word "growth"—that this science is best applied in the "growth phase" or to grow one's customer base.

Is this how you think of it?

The legitimate question; therefore, is **when, within a journey of inventing innovative products or services, is growth hacking of the highest value to apply?**

And on top of that, is growth hacking meant to focus on product scale alone?

The way I apply growth hacking; and therefore, what I advise as an entrepreneur, startup investor and University Instructor who has **lived** growth hacking for nearly two decades, is to apply "growth hacking" from two perspectives—which I like to visualize with the following diagram:

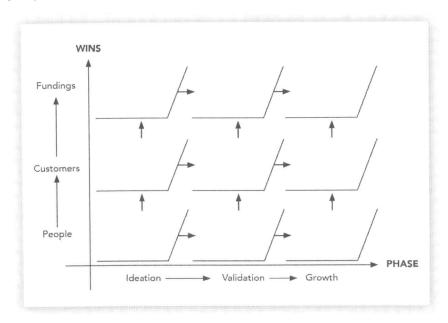

The **PHASE** in which the company is in, we put on an X-axis.

I) Ideation
II) Validation
III) Growth

The **WINS,** which the company requires, we put on the Y-Axis.

I) People
II) Customers
III) Funding

When we think about the startup journey, we can break it down into three separate **Phases**: A beginning, middle, and an end. Therefore, on the X-axis of the above diagram, we see these three phases: The beginning phase being **Ideation**, the middle being **Validation**, and the final phase of **Growth**.

Within these phases and located, then, on the Y-axis of the above diagram, we have what I like to call **Wins**, which are to be seen as "fundamental wins" over time. Within each "win," startups have "key tasks" that help move the needle from one phase to the next.

What are some **Wins** that are the key ingredients of a startup?

GROWTH HACKING WINS (Y-axis):

First—and most fundamentally—is **People**. People, by the way, does not just include the founding team; people actually includes the developers, designers, product managers and marketers who all-together contribute in building the product. So within this key responsibility of obtaining people, there are included those who build the product, the mid-management team, and the core team, which as a result leads to "having the product" itself, then leading you to your next fundamental win:

AKA the **Customers** (the obvious wins), which then—and of course, if you have no customers, you get no funds—leads to **Funding**, which actually is not a goal but a necessity for product-focused startups that want to scale fast.

Now, back to the question on when in this startup journey it is best to apply Growth Hacking:

The great news is that growth hacks apply for each of these **Wins** within each **Phase** of your startup journey! Yes, I know, the obvious application is for customer wins, but one can take it beyond, into winning new team members as well as applying for fundraising activities.

The Essential **WINS** are:

1) GROWTH HACK PEOPLE = Build a team

To find **People**, you not only need an ongoing outreach recruiting activity, but also continuous awareness and visibility! Startups need to act out of the box in order to attract the best team.

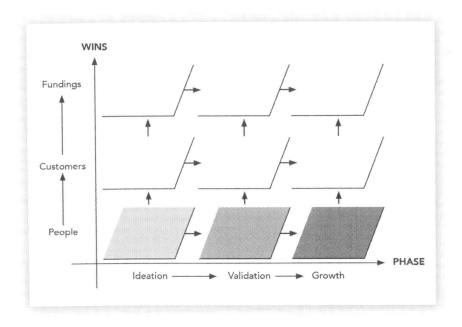

Founding Team:

The typical question you hear around the founding team is "**Where do I find my co-founder?**"

Either you are dead lucky and were in Kindergarten, Elementary, Middle, High School or College with your Co-Founder, where you've known them for so many years you don't have to growth hack anything.... Or you are in a situation where you are seeking your co-founder.

If not co-founders then Engineers, Product & Design, S&M, Operations, Finance, and Customer Success.

Especially when you are in Silicon Valley, the challenge is to find your team members.

Obviously, if you have raised the dollars, then you don't need to find the hack, because you can pay them. But if you don't have the dollars, then you have to get creative, working with low resources to find your talent.

Where do you find the talent?

This is one of the problems you can solve by leveraging platforms such as LinkedIn, AngelList, MeetUp.com, and others where you can automate outreach activities by using tools, copy and resources that put your work on steroids—pretty similar approach as the strategy called CAB described in a few chapters. By doing so, one increases reach, expanding their network and the probability of finding their team.

2) GROWTH HACK CUSTOMERS = Get Traction

Then, the obvious growth hacking purpose you can use is growth hacking for the **Customer**. This is the obvious one, right?

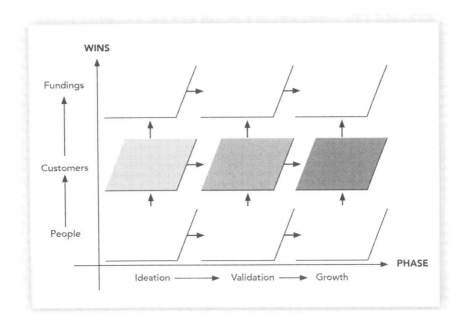

How do you use growth hacks for customers?

You are invited to read a series of example hacks throughout this book on how to win customers; however, as shown on the above diagram, keep in mind that a great entrepreneur doesn't apply Growth Hacking only for obtaining customers.

3) GROWTH HACK FUNDING = Raise Dollars

And last but not least—and maybe the less known application but a compelling one—is to use growth hacking to stand apart in your **Fundraising activities** as differing from the norm.

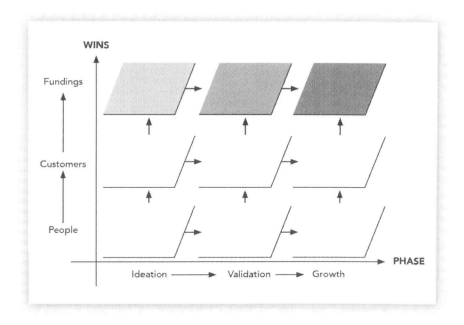

Given that this growth hacking usage is known to raise the most FAQs, I'll share one common hack right away on how to raise a Seed round:

Seed rounds are formed by angel investors.

But who is an angel investor other than Ron Conway, Tim Draper, and Paul Graham (top 3 in 2017)?

Now, either your target must include angel investors, though they are few and havealy targeted, or you will have to focus on "first time" angel investors who have some dollars in the bank and would like to gain access to startups.

Let me phrase this another way: Angel investors are often vice-presidents who simply make enough income during the month to become an angel investor, without really considering themselves as such.

Now, having identified this angel investor persona, the question is: How to scale and get to more of these personas?

Well, you can use LinkedIn; for instance: You filter your search results based on title and industry—industry being tied to your industry, so that the person you're going to connect with will have an affinity and understanding for your startup; what you are doing. Then you start targeting directors, CEO's, Vice Presidents, Senior Vice Presidents, and you use copy that makes it feel exclusive for them to engage with.

Once you have an investor contact, you learn that investors want to connect the dots.

Meaning, they won't invest at a first meeting. Instead of sending "update emails," a simple hack to run towards investors is to add a pixel in a link you send the investor (to click on your video, demo or deck)—by using tools like pixelme.me or Quokka, for which you can then use retargeting ads against it. Meaning that whenever an investor gets an email from you, and clicks on your PDF for instance, he/she now keeps on seeing your advertisement leveraged by the retargeting ad network.

P.S. Ideally you would like to show your growth charts!

Obviously the more money you raise, the less growth hacks you'll have to run as you'll be able to spend more of your dollars accelerating wins.

The takeaway here is that you can growth hack on every single of those **Wins**, for every single **Phase**!

As Growth Hacking is the art of taking innovation to market by leveraging new tools and creative tactics, startups go through three PHASES and require three essential WINNING ingredients.

Growth Hacking helps to accelerate pipeline growth and conversion rates of potential "WINS" from the ideation phase, over to validation, to growth and company exit.

Meaning, depending on the needs of each phase, growth hacking takes you to:

More PEOPLE wins | More CUSTOMER wins | More FUNDING wins

4 - HOW TO APPLY GROWTH HACKING

We must put as much innovation in our Go-To-Market strategy as we do in the creation of our product. Please read this sentence again. Do not stop your creativity at product-level (aka building things), but take that creativity into your go-to-market (aka how to hook customers). These are the two halves to a whole, successfully accepted product.

Whenever you build a new product, you need to get to PMF. [Product/Market Fit: when your product satisfies market demands.]

Most products in the MVP phase (the majority of all startups) struggle big time to get customer interest when they hit the market. Without customer or user support, most products never get off the ground, and thus have no basis upon which to build a product/market fit.

So many startups start guessing and throwing things at their product as they have weak ground to springboard from; no customer-centric direction.

So, here is where Growth Hacking comes into play.

To get to PMF in this age of blockchain, AI and robotics, you constantly need to be utilizing cutting edge tools.

Don't allow fear, insecurity, or the need for some "limited number of validation" to inhibit you from strategizing your audience for your GTM.

A pitfall I often see in early startups is procrastination of the GTM strategy. Don't wait until your product is complete to begin strategizing. So long as you have an assumption for your target audience, you can begin to craft your strategy, and get a head start on the process… or rather, as I like to say, **start before you start**.

Are you hoping to have a tech product on the market that aims to have big-time traction?

Then put the same creativity, engagement, and passion into your GTM as you do into your product. Don't just utilize IP [intellectual property] in your product, but build it into your GTM strategy, hereby making you unique.

You need to have a clear path when it comes down to how to get traction.

I have built a roadmap of the three main pillars growth hacking is built upon: The pathway to success, which I share with you so you can start applying it in your venture.

The Three Pillars are:

The Painkiller Exercise. How to convey your product is a painkiller rather than a vitamin. The way you say things either makes others buy into what you do, or not. **Communication** is the fundamental first step to Growth Hacking.

Recalibrating Your Mindset. Are you approaching the market in a way that makes your target audience want to "buy in" or are you just another product trying to be sold? **Tactical promotions**—with a built--in, compelling "painkiller"—are 75% of growth hacking.

Executing Coherently. And ultimately in Growth Hacking, how does your funnel look? What is the journey you'd like your customer to experience? Talking about experience, what are the **Tools and Tactics** you are implementing at every single funnel stage for your persona to have fun engaging with?

Every single time you get in contact with your buyer persona, the touchpoints (emails, website contact, etc.) must be unique.

The three ways in which growth hacking activities can help you stand out:

1. You need to catch them by surprise.

Catch your persona in a *wow* moment, somehow where they don't expect you to touch base with them. Perhaps through a new tool, rather than using traditional methods such as email lists and website prompts. Your buyer persona will be more willing to engage when approached in a fresh way, leading to a wow moment where they feel unbridled in their pursuit of your product.

2. You need to use tools that make engaging a different experience than with usual startups.

The buyer persona brain closes down to the experiences that are obviously ads or asking for something. On the other hand, buyers may not even notice that they are interacting with you when you use tools and tactics that catch them off guard. Provide your persona with a smooth journey, by creating an experience people have fun engaging with, and they will sign up without feeling the pain of traditional advertisement.

3. You need to say things that make the persona curious to engage with you and your product.

Rather than plain sales or marketing tactics, where the buyer persona recognizes, *Oh, well, this is another product seeking wins*, you convey the product in a way that speaks to your persona and intrigues them. You use words that speak to your persona's interest, grabbing their interest first, before trying to engage them.

As a first, quick assessment, ask yourself the following three questions:

1. Are we using a channel (such as email) that most other startups are using too?

- Or, can we find *alternative channels* that are less cluttered?

2. Are we forcing users and visitors through boring sign-up forms?

- Or, can we use tools and widgets that hook our customers through fun interaction?

3. Is the language we are using going ignored by our customers?

- Or, is it intriguing, raising the curiosity for our readers to take action?

"Innovation Without Execution is an Illusion"

5 - WHO IS IT FOR

Growth Hacking is for tech entrepreneurs with an idea, early stage startups wanting to validate their idea, prototype or MVP, or intrapreneurs working within corporations who are looking to validate their product before taking it to market.

Growth hacking is primarily used for two reasons, whether via entrepreneurs or intrapreneurs:

    a) to get validation and generate momentum

    b) to find a repeatable process

The art of Growth Hacking is best when applied by one of two personas:

THE OBVIOUS: For a Startup Entrepreneur

THE NOT-SO-OBVIOUS: For a Corporate Intrapreneur

Let us start with sussing out **the obvious**.

A startup entrepreneur lives within the mindset of a lean startup (to build a product that some customer wants); therefore, growth hacking becomes the Go-To Tactic for validation and growth. Startup entrepreneurs aim to develop products people want, and often in order to bring them to market, this lean mindset applies not only to product development, but as well to the go-to-market strategy.

Growth hacking is a lean activity, as well as a fresh, new approach, because of its continuously new tools, quickened pace, and how it requires more out-of-the box execution than traditional sales and marketing.

Within this **obvious use for entrepreneurs**, growth hacking can be applied to two different startup stages:

1A, Obvious Use: Post PMF to scale

1B, Less Obvious Use: To get validation and generate momentum

But because growth hacking includes the word *growth*, people often associate it as something you **only** run to scale or grow the company, aka once you find product market fit.

However, this is not true.

1A, Obvious Use: Post-PMF to Scale

For application of scaling the Go-To-Market. This is the entrepreneur who has a product on the market, has achieved product/market fit, and now would like to get into a repeatable process.

So, if you are an entrepreneur and you've achieved early product/market fit, you are then experimenting **to find a repeatable process** and a way of having reduced CAC [Customer Acquisition Costs]; but, at the same time, with exponential growth. This is absolutely what growth hacking is for, and definitely the most obvious and widely accepted use of it.

Why?

Because you need to grow your pipeline and funnel quickly in order to have enough leads to successfully bring your product to market!

You get out of the pipeline what you put into the pipeline.

Meaning, the Goal of a Startup in the Post-PMF Phase is to Find a Repeatable Process by Leveraging Growth Hacking.

1B, Less Obvious Use: To Get Validation and Generate Momentum

This is the entrepreneur who has read the book on lean startups, and conducts focus groups, gathering a small amount of people who offer feedback during product development, in order to assess validation.

I see this become a major pitfall with entrepreneurs all the time, where they are only **leveraging a small group of people** for their feedback, causing:

   a) their results to be very biased, as they have interviewed too small of a group, and

b) the entrepreneur's thus feels satisfied by the sheer ability of having reached a small group.

In this case, they do not try to push themselves **beyond their comfort zone** to navigate or embark on activities that help them touch a broader group of potential prospects.

Entrepreneurs must become bold and fierce in their pursuit of execution. You only get to a quality customer through testing with a quantity. In other words, you only get to quality when you use quantity in your GTM. Your product will die with a small quantity, and never see the quality come to pass.

If you have an activity that only approaches a small amount of people (with the *excuse* of getting feedback), then the probability of the entrepreneur's mindset to feel comfortable just doing "smaller" outreaches is true, and vice versa. Many entrepreneurs are too scared to roll out automated activities that create hundreds of daily touchpoints!

So, why would you do something with only a small amount of people, when you *could* create an activity that draws in a larger amount of people?

You wouldn't! You shouldn't. More people leads to more validation; to a large community of potential customers craving for your product, more pre-sales, more referrals, more feedback (aka validation) and ultimately, more success. So the real point of interest here, is the **capability of growth**.

Growth hacking allows you to easily create tactics that give you the option to talk to or work with an exponential amount of people for the same, if not less, effort.

An entrepreneur in this situation is looking for the *secret sauce* that will aid in validation and momentum, and I actually really love when growth hacking is used for these purposes.

Running growth hack tactics to validate ideas and MVPs leads to momentum.

It gives you an expanded understanding of whether you are going in the right direction, through the tremendously important side effect that every prospect you connect to in this phase is one of your product's potential future customers. If they love your product, they will become fans, bringing you new customers.

Growth Hacking Early on Takes You Beyond Small Group User Testing, Towards More Momentum and Validation.

Or... do you already have enough momentum?

What's a good tactic to use to get momentum and validation early on?

Here's an example:

One of the strategies I advise to startups I mentor who are engineered towards B2B [startups that drive revenue through enterprises] is called CAB Strategy [Customer Advisory Board Strategy]. This is where you approach corporate executives—Director level, VP level, C level—who have enough knowledge in the industry you are working in to potentially benefit you in three ways:

1) You pick their brains by making them advisors because they know the industry, and thus can guide you through product development and give you validation if you're headed the right way.

2) To become your early adaptors by becoming your champion, and pushing the innovation internally.

3) Lastly, to become your angel investors.

But **how** can you approach them using growth hacks?

1) Create a top 50 list of *the* largest enterprise brands in your industry (this list must be industry specific) that you would love to work with, if you had the choice to do so.

2) Within this list of top 50 brands, you search at least three personas from different business units, or from different roles, potentially always working from the top down. Start with C level, Senior VP level, or at least the director level, as these individuals will still be dealing with the responsibilities of budget, people and strategy. [You always need these three aspects to make something happen within a company.] Ideal roles are "head of innovation", or Dir/VP of the department you solve a problem for.

3) Then you use outsourcing platforms such as Fiverr or Upwork to hire lead generation freelancers to find these people's names for you (which this—to find specific freelancers—is a hack in its own right).

4) Then, once you find these three people from each of your fifty brands, you can import this list into tools such as GPZ for LinkedIn, or LinkedHelper. What you import is the LinkedIn Profile URLs of the personas you want to get in contact with. The tools allow you to automate activities such as outreach or follow-ups.

This way, instead of sending out three or four emails (what most entrepreneurs tend to do), you have 150 contacts, right there.

This activity is both targeted and personal at the same time. Yet, it could be even larger.

What's important is that you perform this *tactic* on a daily basis, so you get into this movement of understanding the flow of reaching out to market influencers daily.

This, really, is a mindset thing... **recalibrating your mindset**. You change your mindset, where every day, you reach out to your market.

When you start building a pipeline in an activity on a daily basis, and reach out on a daily basis, this increases the probability of your getting validation, thus leading to momentum, by signing LOIs [Letters of Intent], pre-sign ups to participate, POCs, etc! One metric I apply in the startups I mentor is to encourage the founders to reach out to 250 contacts per day, per founder.

Now you are in a situation where you can go to investors and pitch events, and say "well, we have the top directors, VP-level, and C-level for the following brands in the United States as Advisors, Customers, and Angel Investors" and then apply this to your startup traction metrics.

PS: the key to this CAB Strategy is in how you communicate and what promotion you embed into your strategy.

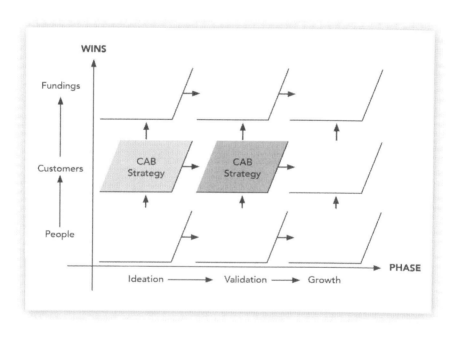

Growth hacking allows you to do more with less. It leverages tools and tactics to find more qualified people with a similar investment in time, so you can put more activities on autopilot. The beauty of this is, by having more people involved, more people are already part of your funnel, meaning: **Once you launch your product, you already have people craving what you do.**

Instead of just 10 people gathered for a focus group, you now have 100, 1,000, maybe 1,000,000 people!

2, Not-So-Obvious Use:
Executives Validating Ideas

The persona most people do not think of is the *intrapreneur*. This includes all executives or individuals within corporations who wish to validate their assumptions before moving forward with their product to market.

The intrapreneur within a corporation who wants to validate their hypothesis will look to growth hacking tactics, which then leads them through a process equal to what the entrepreneur does [see 1A + 1B].

In my Corporate Innovation talks around the globe, within the top three FAQ's I receive is: *How to drive innovation from within, given there is corporate overhead, and executives can't move as fast, or lean, as startup entrepreneurs?*

Intrapreneurs, similar to Entrepreneurs, have to solve a real problem.

Step number one, to start out, is to build a team (for intrapreneurs—these are colleagues who believe in the mission). A wrong expectation from executives becoming intrapreneurs is to raise money for the project/prototype, instead of building a team *first*.

It is exactly in this "team-building" phase, where intrapreneurs need to validate their assumptions, by reaching out to their potential target audience to collect evidence and knowledge to support their case, ultimately making the team fall in love with the problem they are solving.

Evidences can have a variety of faces. Feedback forms, polls, sign-ups, LOIs…. To get there, entrepreneurs and intrapreneurs alike decide whether to a) get just ten opinions from peers (mostly biased), or b) approach the market in a broader scale to not only brings in more results, but also—and most relevantly—to transform your mindset to execute things that lead to broader market penetration, capitalization, and ultimately… wins!

This also answers the question of how a corporation can benefit from growth hacking.

So, **executive entrepreneurs, aka intrapreneurs**, please see 1A and 1B, change your mindset, build a team, and validate your assumptions.

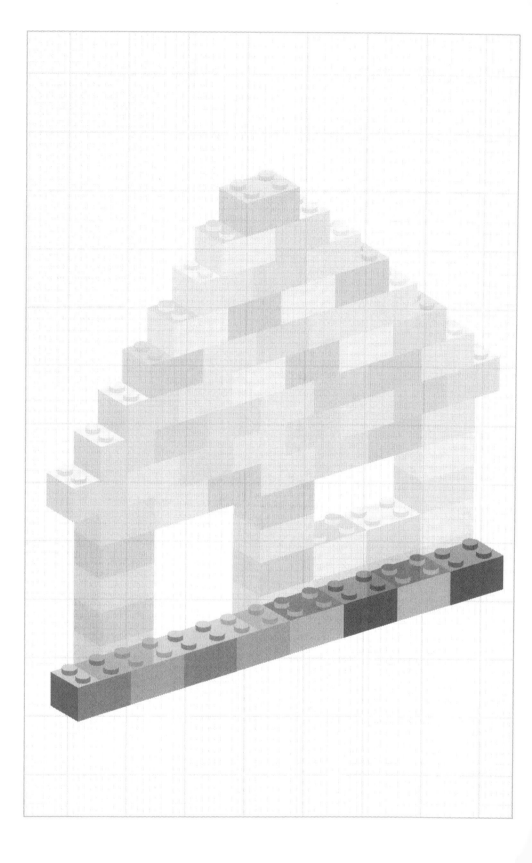

PILLAR ONE

CONVEYING PRODUCT VALUE: THE NUANCES OF COMMUNICATION

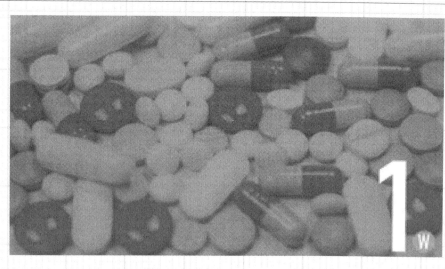

Are you conveying to be a vitamin or a painkiller?

1 – THE NUANCES OF COMMUNICATION

The foundation of growth hacking upon which these three pillars are built is: **Communication**.

It may seem simple, but in my experience, the startup entrepreneurs I meet are speaking way too generally. Generally, meaning, too vague, wishy washy, or nebulous about the problem they are actively solving.

I often ask them *why* they are speaking so generically about what they do.

What are you doing **exactly**? *What problem are you solving: For whom, and by leveraging what?*

Especially in this startup age, people don't communicate their value clearly enough, and don't convey in a tangible way *what* they are doing, and *for whom*.

Most entrepreneurs tend to say *what we do is all for everybody*. So general, so general! Too general, in fact.

Some bad examples:

a) "Our platform helps students find deals."

b) "Our app creates a personalized shopping experience."

c) "Our API connects with other tools to push data."

The reason this will lead to low engagement is it describes features, rather than benefits. Imagine this value proposition on an add, email, or social post. You think this is something people have never heard of or read before? Or does this positioning sound similar to something you have already seen or heard before?

Well, this is exactly how most potential customers are reacting to 90% of these adds:

"Uff, another one of these! Seen it already! No interest."—*click*, *delete*.

In other words, you know what the result of this is?

You have *way less* engagement, because it is not clear **what the thing does** and **for whom specifically it is of value**.

You start becoming just another "me too" product.

And while, of course, we can understand this to a point—we see a competitor dominating a market we know we can rock and want a piece of the action—it doesn't gain traction easily. When you are just another "me too" product, where people don't tend to engage.

You can try to apply growth hack tools, but if you don't have a clear communication and value proposition—a clear USP [Unique Selling Proposition]—on **how** you are different, and **to whom** you are different, then it doesn't help you to use the tools, because you will still drive low engagement.

You need a unique trait to target to your audience. And what makes you unique? Trigger-Based Communication.

Trigger based Communication is essential to growth hacking your startup, because it's the foundation for how you gain persona attention.

How can you expect people to care about you if they aren't hooked on what you do, and how you can help them specifically?

You need to find the root of their pain, and be able to communicate specifically on **how** you cure it.

This, they will remember. This, they will feel when they experience their pain, and are triggered to seek you and your business out!

Communication is the vehicle through which you transmit strategy.

Now, what is the difference between strategy and communication?

Communication is more about the words you select; whereas, Strategy, or in other words Promotion, is more about the way in which you package those words for your target audience.

The gold isn't found by merely saying things and conveying values—but in **how** you are saying the things you do. Which tone you use; what words you select. Your brand is the sum of all sentences you publish.

Your target audience puts you in a box based on what they read. Meaning, if your lingo is technical, then you attract only technical people. If you use a language that is very "promotional", then people who want to make a deal will engage.

I'm almost nerdy in this exercise. Given I speak six languages, I enjoy measuring the "weight of words" by A/B testing different vocabularies to see how the market interacts.

What I've learned, especially since living in Silicon Valley, is that you don't "sell to a customer" when running a startup. Rather, startups grow faster when you "make the persona part of the product".

This might also be tied to the fact that the baby boomer generation were more into i) structure and ii) formalities, while millennials and especially generations z and y, "connect" using a different "tone". A tone where formalities convey "complications and efforts", while a "spoken" lingo conveys "authenticity and accessibility" which stands on "transparency—and today, it's all about that.

A couple of examples heretofore:

WEAK:

"I would like to meet to demo our product"

TRY INSTEAD

"I want to **pick your brain** on what we are building"

WEAK

Our company works with developers to distribute their apps

TRY INSTEAD

We **collaborate** with developers to drive market reach

WEAK

Sign up for our newsletter

TRY INSTEAD

Get it directly into your inbox

However, the core difference between Communication and Promotion is, when including promotion, I define before I communicate, and I think the entire key to successful communication is based on **defining the strategy of communication**.

Are you using strategy when you communicate?

Strategy is the big picture. You cannot think about communication without your strategy.

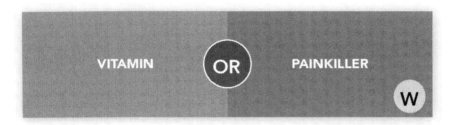

Hey, what is it you do? is the core of Communication—**to whom do you provide value, and how do you express it?**

Promotion / Strategy is the way in which you approach Communication.

2 - THE RAPID ASSESSMENT EXERCISE: HOW ARE YOU DIFFERENT

So what I have here is a six step approach to help you recognize *how you are different*; a process to help you uncover how you can become a painkiller.

It's a very simple approach that I use to lead almost every single startup I work with, usually after we create the business canvas strategy. The business canvas strategy is a more detailed exercise which I teach classes on. This strategy requires the entrepreneurs to dig in with more detail, which is the reason why I came up with a faster version of it, called the **Rapid Value Assessment Exercise**.

It allows you to rapidly assess your value proposition / how you are different.

First, we analyze the competition, asking who our competitor is. You always have competition; if you don't have competition, you don't have a business. The minimum competition you have is the status quo.

So, you analyze your competition and understand what they are conveying—what's their **value proposition**? Once you understand what their value proposition is, you ask who they are serving.

Then you start doing your homework, and you say *well, whom am I serving*?

Who is *my* target audience, and *how am I different*?

I am going to emphasize here that this means: **How am I five to ten times different than the status quo / my competition?**

For certain, when we talk about innovation, if you are not five to ten times more different, then basically why are you doing it? If you are not five to ten times different, you are a "me too" product, and then you have challenges in gaining attention.

Once you figure out how you are five to ten times different, then you start saying to yourself, "well, how **relevant** are these differences to my target audience?"

Relevant, meaning, what you are solving, and the way you are solving it. Is this super relevant, aka high on a scale from 1-10, or is it just nice to have (aka on the lower scale of 1-10)? And then, you start being very honest with yourself, and say, "Ok, what I created—this differentiation—is it **relevant to my target audience?**"

Then, you move into the next step by asking yourself, "How is my difference relevant to my target audience? Is this very relevant; of *crucial relevance* to my target audience?"

Is it a vitamin or a painkiller?

In any case, this exercise leads to a fast self-reflection of where you stand in your value proposition, but I suggest every entrepreneur do the exercise of the value proposition design—which by the way is a subset of the lean business canvas strategy—at least once.

And once you've moved through this entire six step approach, you can craft your value proposition, which is basically the fundament for growth hacking.

For an example of how to fill out this form for your own uses, you would say something like the following:

Unlike [some competitor], Our [tool/app/program] helps [for example, teachers] who want [their students to become aware of the relative market] by [replacing old teaching methods] and [gaining purpose, while also having fun in career counseling]. Our product helps someone do something… and so on and so forth.

It's super clear. In this section of the book we are talking about communication and, to be clear, this is a quick assessment. Words count… so this is what you have to say.

And now, you're ready to move on to the **Painkiller Exercise**.

Six Step Approach on How to Become a Painkiller:

1. List out the competition by name.

2. What is their core value proposition?

- "We do *this* for them by providing *this*."

3. Who is their main target group?

4. What is your main target group?

5. What makes you stand out? (5-10 examples)

- How you are different, faster, cheaper, better....

6. Rate how much your target audience craves your USP on a scale from 1-6.

THEN you can Craft Your Core Value Proposition.

You need to understand how you are unique, because when you growth hack, the message you have to convey is **we are unique**. Otherwise, you basically do not get high conversion rates, and growth hacking is all about those high conversion rates!

Lesson One Takeaway: Prepare to Convey to Whom You are Unique.

This is pretty important. Why? Because now we finally understand what we are!

It may seem pretty basic, but I see startups overlook this aspect of themselves all the time without even realizing it.

It's all about being honest with yourself about what you do, and then problem solving to get to where you need to be, to **be unique to your target audience.**

Now, imagine, tomorrow morning, by coincidence, the two of us meet at the coffee shop, and I ask you, "Hey, <name>, what is it that you do?"

And now it's your turn. It's your moment, where you can convey either in a very complicated way what you do, or you use the **Painkiller Exercise** to craft a value proposition that makes me say, "Hey, let's stay in touch. I want to hear more about this."

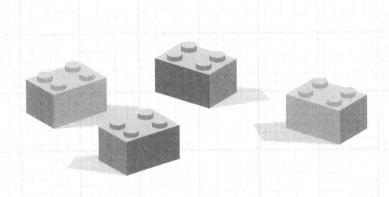

> "Prepare to Convey to Whom You are Unique."
>
> #metoosucks

3 - TRIGGER BASED MARKETING

How do you communicate?

Trigger-based marketing is when you reach out to your persona—whether through ads, email, your website, or whatever—phrasing things in a way which would **trigger** them to take action on your product.

Trigger-based marketing is the assessment of how people perceive what you say. Not just the value, but also the aspect of how you have access to it.

What are the trigger words that cause an action to take place from your buyer persona?

Do you have a series of custom triggers within your copy to prompt the person to feel inclined to take action?

I've learned that you have the best conversion rates when using a minimum of three to five triggers in your copy, regardless of whether it's email, ads, whatever.

So what are a couple of those triggers?

Here's an example of trigger-based marketing. The purpose of the product referenced here is to "connect executives from corporations with startups".

Most people would simply say, "connecting executives and startups", which sounds great as a slogan, but do we get enough conversion rates from it?

Now, let's break down the **trigger-based approach** by analyzing the following five triggers, and how you see them being utilized in the copy on this landing page.

Trigger-Based Marketing Tactics Used Here:

1) Scarcity Strategy
2) Limitation
3) Geo-trigger
4) Limit by Industry
5) Limit by Job Position

Step number one, as a title, you have "invitation only." Meaning what? Meaning that whatever you're about to read, you only would have access to if you have been invited. This psychologically causes the reader to maintain interest. Fear of missing out. Intrigue. This creates the first craving feeling, where actually, without knowing what it is, the reader starts to want to be a part of whatever it is you're offering.

Why? Because it is invitation only.

Now, before I move on, one of the key things I so often hear, especially with product/engineer founders, is, " Tommaso, we have a platform, and this platform can be used by everybody, everywhere, in every way. So we don't need to say, "invite only" and limit our audience.

Well, guess what? What we are trying to craft here is not the engineering itself, but a tactic to increase how many people are signing up to actually engage with your product.

Therefore, "invitation only" creates a craving. I also call this **scarcity strategy**, and often say "invite only" as well as limiting the amount of brands I use, making it a *double scarcity strategy*.

Now, to move on, the second part: "10". Not only do we have the limitation of "invite only", but we also say that only the first ten who have been invited will have the luxury; the probability of getting to experience the thing. Thus, you're adding double the pressure onto the individual to interact.

What does it cause? It causes the reader to say, "I don't have time to waste. If I want to act and shoot for my chance of engagement, I have to act now. Why? Because there's only ten welcome.

So now, not only are we using scarcity strategy, but now we are also using the **strategy of limitation**. I will be digging in even deeper to these strategies in the next pillar.

The third trigger: "New York". This is a **location-based trigger**. If I, the reader, am in New York, I presume this ad is talking to me. It allows the reader to already feel emotionally connected to the event, based on their geo-location, and makes them think they have a good shot at engagement.

The next trigger is to do with **industry**: "retail". The word "retail" narrows the search again, where if you are in retail in New York, you're gonna say, "This is talking to me!"

The fifth trigger of "executives" defines the **title/role**, meaning, when you start your outreach, you are using a filter to narrow interest.

These people for whom this ad is engineered feel hooked.

Now, why are most entrepreneurs not doing this? Because this requires effort and being very detailed and methodical. In fact, if you take a look at some of my metrics (I create sheets based on industries, where I combine the industries with the roles and location to see the overlap), within every single cell of this sheet, I have a custom phrase I use to connect to every single custom target audience that I am trying to attract, whether on Facebook, Adwords or LinkedIn.

Let's take a step back for a minute, to give you an example.

- Version one: You send an email that says, "I would like you to connect startups with executives."
- Version number two, assuming your target audience reader is an executive working in retail in New York, they receive a message saying, "You've been invited. But only the first ten retail executives in New York can take action. So I thought you might want to chat."

Which would you engage with? Ok, I can hear your thoughts. You're thinking, "Well obviously the second one, Tommaso."

My question for you is, "If it is so obvious, why aren't you doing it?"

You have to play with words to cause your persona to crave interaction with your product!

The probability of your persona taking action is much higher if you phrase your copy in this way, instead of something too general.

Rather than something that sounds more like a slogan, **be specific; be methodical.** Conversion rates are not a coincidence. There is a math to it, and I hope this process can help you craft something more tangible.

Psychology shows that the pain of losing something is much bigger, and makes you feel more than the joy of having something. You don't sell a product, you sell an experience. People don't buy things, they buy what those things do with them.

So, if all of this is true, then the question becomes, "How can we do things with our buyer persona?"

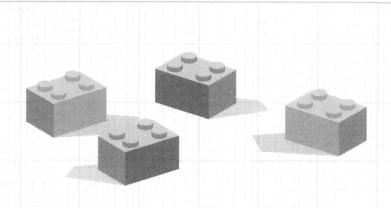

"Growth Hacking is the Use of Triggers Within the Communication that Cause Your Persona to Want to Take Action. Applying Trigger-Based Communication is 60% of Growth Hacking."

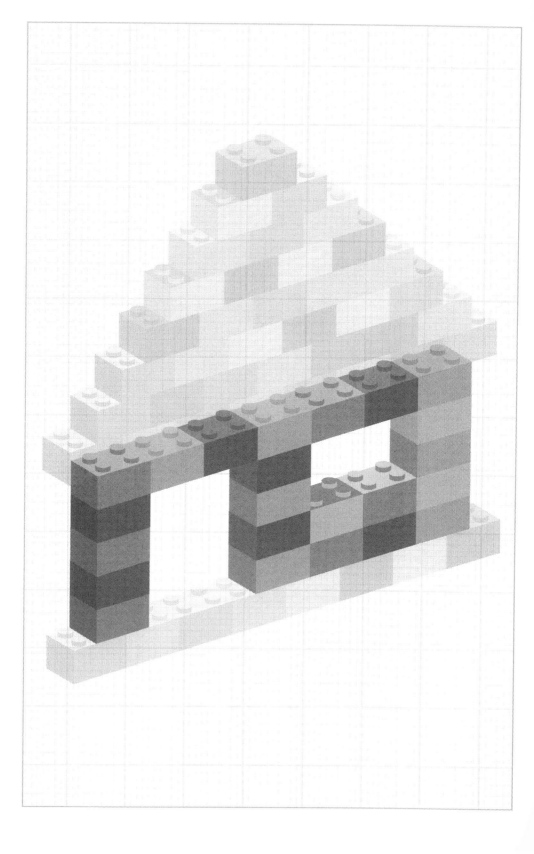

PILLAR TWO

RECALIBRATE YOUR MINDSET: THE PROMOTIONAL STRATEGIES THAT LEAD TO CRAVING FANS

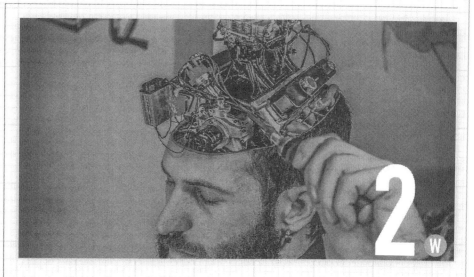

What does it mean to Recalibrate Your Mindset?

It means, basically, that you have to rethink what you know about sales and marketing. Traditional sales and marketing are still valid. But in the age of next-gen technologies, such as AI, computer advancement, and VR/AR, just to name a few, the way you bring products to market must be rethought.

Growth hacking is the agile, contemporary approach at targeting your audience.

How do you bring your product to market? How do you package it? What is, strategically, the approach you offer the product?

This is why we call this strategic promotion. We're going to take a look at eight examples of strategic promotions that make a total difference when offering something to your target audience. These eight examples recalibrate your mindset to convey your offering in an appealing way, where people say, "Yes I want it!"

1 - START BEFORE YOU START

Here is the first strategic promotion I share with you. I love the concept of it: **Starting before you start**. Let me tell you what it is.

The typical pitfall I see most startups fall into is they start building a product and doing some initial focus groups, and they think once they release the product it will go viral, and that *once it goes viral*, they can attach a traditional go-to-market strategy to it.

At the end of the day, however; what happens is that the MVP sucks (the first MVP always sucks), and it doesn't go viral. And then, once you—in a panic—realize you had better bring your product to market, you find that you actually have no time, no money, and if you're unlucky enough, no team.

So how do you start before you start?

I want to give you an example.

My most recent startup—my fourth—was an app called SWAAAG, that basically connected kids and fans with their influencers.

Now, this was at a time where Snapchat had not raised their A-round yet; it was at a time when Instagram was purely about pictures and no video, and there were almost no video apps or tools on the market, save for YouTube's long-format video and the freshly launched Vine app, focused on 6-second video clips.

So I said to myself, "Well, what if I create an app that allows teenagers to interact by sharing thrilling moments, and allows them to express how much they like one another's videos… only instead of how the others are doing it, I use a sticker concept in which every sticker has a particular value/weight…?"

So I decided to use stickers ranging from 1 to 1000, where people could say how much they loved a video using this broad-scale sticker system. For example, using a sticker in the form of a kiss, an Oscar, a heart, or a kitten, any user could rate another user's video while expressing how they felt about it. A leaderboard, then, would show the top ten best-ranked videos.

Remember, this was my fourth startup, meaning I'd had two exits already. The reason I mention this is because I had a couple startups-worth of experiences, and a few dollars in my bank account.

What I **could have done**, was to start developing the prototype. I had enough knowledge, know-how, and money to move forward with the creation of the tool, **but I didn't**.

What I did instead was, I started validating all my assumptions **without a product!**

What were my assumptions?

1) There was space available next to Instagram and Facebook for another social-oriented app.

2) I had the capability of **finding the right channel**; meaning, how to distribute the product to market in a way that would influence my target audience of kids.

3) As a company, we might have the capability of actually managing and retaining teenagers (provided we know that Generation Y and Generation Z are very, let's say, different and opinionated, compared to others).

Here's how I validated these assumptions without a product:

My goal was to reach out to my target audience. Who was my target audience? Influencers and kids.

I began by reaching out to kids, basically saying "Hey, I'm creating this tool that allows you to share your thrilling moments through video. People can engage with you through your videos, and your influencers will also start connecting with you through this platform, are you interested?"

With this outreach, **I began to form a community**.

Once I had this community, and started verticalizing it, I started reaching out to a few influencers in the United States, as well as in Brazil.

Brazil was the perfect place for me to test my app. I had great access to the market there, could bring them the technology, and thus more easily get influencers on board.

I started talking with a couple of influencers—singers, athletes and such, as it was just before the world cup. They're pretty open to these topics of innovation in Brazil; really, they're pretty open to any technology that comes from the Silicon Valley.

One of the influencers I met in Brazil was in the music industry. I pitched him something like, "Hey do you want to be one of the first ones to join this new video app that facilitates a better experience of connecting you as an influencer with your fans?"

He liked the idea. He was a visionary, and recognized the use of limitation. What we agreed upon was to start creating some videos through the app, as well as post on social media about it, saying, "Hey guys,

I'm one of the first ones using this cool, new app from Silicon Valley, and if you think it's cool too, here's a code you can use **to be the first in line** to get it! *This* is the code you can use."

And he had a **specific code** tied to him.

Now, what is the code exactly? It was a static code that we gave to this specific influencer, because with that code, we could track how much engagement / how many downloads we would have achieved based on this specific musician's outreach.

There was no app, alright? This was me **validating** if I could reach out to influencers, and to my target audience.

I was able to validate, actually, the most challenging thing, because influencers need individual attention. And really, so do teenagers, who are on the other side of that demand.

Once I started to see and understand that there was an interest for the app, I started developing a batch generator, which I published on Google Play and in the App Store. This batch generator app was nothing more than a tool in which the user could insert the code the musician had posted, which then ended up leading them to a screen that said,

"Hey, you're following these influencers right now, and you are Number 23 (or whatever) in getting the official app. Click on this button to share with friends, and share this code to jump up the list and be one of the first to get the app. The more people to request early access using your unique link pushes you higher and higher up the list."

SWAAAG EARLY ACCESS PROMO   ANOTHER EXAMPLE

That's what I call creating **scarcity.** The same idea as applied to the example on trigger-based marketing I shared with you at the end of the last pillar.

The Psychology behind the scarcity strategy is, instead of just offering the product (meaning "hey this is what we do"), you make the product rare, so your target audience starts craving for it, as this implies that it isn't for everybody; meaning, it's limited, and therefore your persona wants to be part of it.

This is a strategic promotion that triggers, when used aptly, the persona to engage, as they don't want to miss out. To put it simply, if you only offer something, I can decide whether I want to take it. But if you make the offering rare, I will feel compelled to secure it, to ensure I get it.

And to go back to my story, in that specific moment **I still had no product.** This was just about validation.

So, what assumptions exactly did I end up validating?

1) I am capable of reaching out to an influencer to get his or her involvement.

2) The target persona (aka influencer) was hooked enough that they were ready to take action (aka post and share the video/code).

3) The target persona (aka users) were open to add another app to their screen (which is definitely not a simple endeavor).

Within just a couple of days, I had a notable amount of downloads—over 3000—and still with zero product.

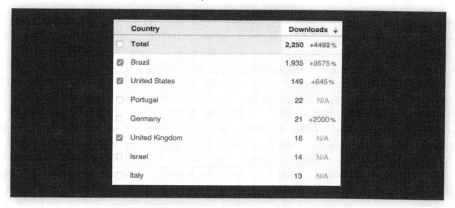

And by the way, the nice side-effect we experienced based upon these results was that we were capable of closing a seed round, and yes without a product!

Now, how did that happen?

When I flew back to Silicon Valley from my trip to alpha-release my product, I went back to speak with a couple of investors (yes, in Silicon Valley you always raise dollars) and the beauty of the trip this time was that I was asked, "Tommaso, what is it that you actually do? That your app does?"

And for the first time in my life, I was able to respond, "I don't know."

And this, what I now call the **I Don't Know Strategy**, causes investors especially to be very surprised.

Why? Because investors are used to hearing these super smart answers from entrepreneurs, and "I don't know" isn't one of them.

What I responded was, "Well, let me expand on why I don't know. I actually don't know what I'm going to do, but I do know what I did, which was the following: I validated my value proposition by reaching out to my target persona. I found this specific niche in my target persona, who were responding positively to my value proposition, and were ready to engage, even without a product. Based on this engagement, we created a small batch which was nothing more than a viral loop built into our app so that we could track where the downloads came from. Within a short period of time, users took action, and now, *here* is the amount of downloads we have so far."

I went on to say, "**By the way,** if you're an investor, we are raising a seed round. Unfortunately, we are over-subscribed; **but**, because it's you, we can still give you a slot to write a check."

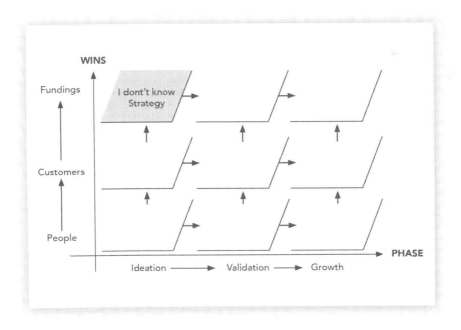

And *that's* how we raised our seed round.

==Now my question to you, the reader, is, how would *you* like to raise dollars without an MVP? Without even having a product?==

Well, in this case, I highly recommend you **start before you start**.

All I had to do was communicate the facts to my investors, and they were in. This is the reason why I vouch that **starting before you start is the most valuable thing you can do for your startup.**

This process will save you a lot of money, a lot of time, and in some cases, marriages and families.

And in this process, **value proposition validation is key.**

And how do you validate value proposition early enough?

By creating a community. Starting a Facebook group. By engaging and learning with the community, making them feel like a part of something, going on speaking engagements, and testing your idea before you have the product.

Test different traction channels, so you can validate the bulk of your idea with your target audience.

Just don't be scared.

Startups come to me all the time, saying, "No, no, no Tommaso, this is not a release…. This is a *silent release.*"

………. ¡#@%*&$!

Um, what the *f*!#* is a silent release?!?!?

I mean, if I ask you whether you want to have a loud release or a silent release, what would you want to have?

A f*cking big bang release, amiright?

The only reason you would have a silent release is if you have **failed in your approach.**

So don't release silently... create a **scarcity strategy**. Make it rare—say, "Hey, we are releasing this, who wants to be part of it?" Create pre-sign-ups before releasing, to gain contacts. Create videos that announce it, like Dropbox was doing before they released.

So in other words, very simply, **you have to generate hype before you release.**

If you're not able to create hype, the probability of your product failing is pretty high, because you are not starting to engage your target audience in your topic soon enough, nor with enough momentum. Thus, who's interested in your product when it releases? No one... heck, maybe you aren't even interested enough yet.

If you **are able to create the hype**, however; then, once you *do* start releasing your product, you will have an existing community of people desiring your product—a lot of cheerleaders; a lot of ambassadors. In this case it is easy to create viral loops to increase your reach, and therefore the probability of your target audience to engage.

Start Before You Start.

2 – DISCOVER THE UNCLUTTERED CHANNEL

The next promotional strategy under the umbrella of **changing your mindset** is to **discover the uncluttered channel.**

What does this mean?

When I ask startups what their go-to-market strategy is, they often say, "Well, once we release the product, we will do something on social media." Or, another one I hear often is, "We will send out emails to our prospects."

These activities are bullsh*t, because 99% of other entrepreneurs are thinking and doing exactly the same. As a consequence, it will get you nowhere.

What I mean by this is, don't start using tools and channels that are also used by most of the other startups on the market. If you do so, the recipient will have a very similar experience with your product as they do with many others on the market. They will recognize the format and check out. This will not lead to high engagement.

I would like to offer you an economic example to make this idea more tangible. Assume you are running a mobile application, and you are trying to achieve the maximum amount of downloads. In order to get the downloads, you think of using Facebook as your traction channel. As a matter of fact, it shows that a mobile download costs usually between $4-8 per active user. Meaning, these are the customer acquisition costs.

Now, assuming that you, as an early stage startup, are not greatly funded, if you embark on this strategy of aiming for downloads by leveraging facebook, you have almost lost before you've started.

Why?

Because we always have competitors with deeper pockets, don't we? And because we have these competitors with deeper pockets, imagine if they use the same Facebook download strategy approach, but they can actually afford it!

Now my question is, who would win in this race of acquiring more downloads? The one with deeper pockets, or you/a traditional startup, which is very budget sensitive? Well, it is the entrepreneur with deeper pockets, obviously.

The question to ask here is, then, why are you embarking on this strategy if you know you cannot outdo your competitor?

Yes, common tools and traction channels are very simple for those who have big pockets, but who of you lean startup entrepreneurs has big dollars in a bank account?

Not many, I'm sure. [Perhaps some intrapreneurs, but you can put your finances to better use by saving them here.]

So what you have to do, to work around the financial barrier, is to rethink this approach.

What you have to do—in terms of recalibrating your mindset—is to **discover new tools,** *weekly.*

Why?!?

Because the new tools lead to an uncluttered channel!

Now the question becomes **where** you can find these tools. You can find and acquire them on platforms such as ProductHunt or BetaRelease.

The beauty of ProductHunt is that you will find tools built by startups, for startups.

Meaning what?

The startups in there are in a similar stage as to where you are, so they would like to gain traction and are more open to collaborate. Secondly, because they are early stage, they are more affordable, and third, they are startups, meaning they are different and should bring innovation to market. Thus, this is exactly where you can find a new method/way/route/path/avenue on how to get to your persona.

And don't tell me that you don't have the time to commit to this practice.

I test at least one to two products every week, and ask me whether I have time? No, I don't. Two kids, a beautiful wife, and a couple startups…. You make the time for things you want to prioritize, and this is a priority. This requires a change of your mindset. A change of your habits to discover weekly new, cool things.

I would like to give you an example on how I growth hacked my blog posts (still found on www.whatittakes.es) years ago.

To start out with, what I wanted to achieve was to share my lessons learned as an entrepreneur with other entrepreneurs. Meaning, my target audience was other entrepreneurs. My product was content. The challenge I had, even back then, was how much quality content there already was in my topic, as offered by such gurus as Steve Blank and Mark Suster, etc.

So, my challenge was to figure out how to start from scratch to build up an audience.

My first step was to understand which topics my readers were currently enjoying.

And based on that, I started to search for a tool, and found Buzzsumo, which helps you find topics based on keywords. In it, you will see how often this topic has been shared through social media. In other words, you find what content is working well, or trending, in your business niche.

I was searching for topics like #entrepreneurship, startups, traction, Y Combinator, etc.... General things in the realm of startup talk, so these were what I searched on Buzzsumo—my hot, new tool.

Why was it important to me?

Because once you see what is trending as a topic, with a tool like this, you can click to see who is actually talking about this topic!

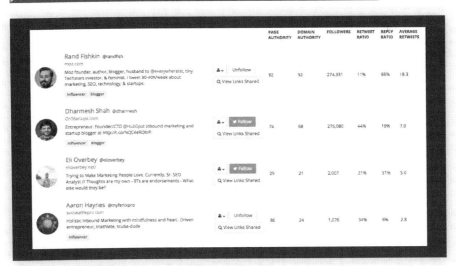

I mean, *wow... awesome!* I have my target audience right there! These are the people I want to have sign-up for my blog!

I had now only one challenge: **How do I get in contact with them?**

There, on Buzzsumo, you can actually expand the results on who has shared the topics you are seeking to find the company name and the individual's full name. The only problem is, there's no listed emails or ways to contact them.

So what I did next was try **to find a tool** to help me find their contact information.

Really, this is what growth hacking is all about. Clumping different things together that, in the end, make sense and lead you towards the goal of converting.

Growth Hacking is not about finding one single tool that brings your GTM from A to Z, but is about slicing your activities into small steps, and for every step, finding the appropriate tools that lead you to your next one. Which, in my case, was then to find the email addresses.

I found a tool called Makesmail that allows you to import individual and company names, and export email addresses to contact them.

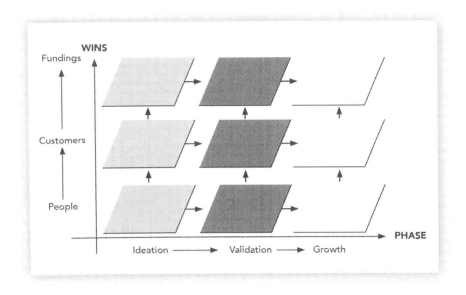

Well, now that I have their email addresses, I'm unstoppable!

So, once you have the email addresses, you start using a very personalized email tool, such as Mailshake.

And here, in this stage, the **content is key.**

I started reaching out to those people who had shared articles and topics about startups, and since I was planning to talk about startups, they really were my ideal target, as influencers, collaborators, etc.

In my email, I said, basically: "Hey you, thanks for sharing what you shared, I learned a lot from it! (Starting with a compliment…) and hey, *by the way*, I'm talking about this too, and thought, because of that, you might be interested in this post, here (including a link). If you feel so called, please share it… and thanks again for sharing your content (another compliment)."

This is my personal outreach, and was a sequence of six emails I put into a cadence and sent to each influencer/collaborator. As a result, I started driving more traffic to the website and converting more and more specifically through this work.

So, the takeaway for this promotional strategy is to **discover and apply an uncluttered channel by leveraging next-gen tools.**

"Growth Hacking is not about finding one single tool that brings your GTM from A to Z, but is about slicing your activities into small steps, and for every step, finding the appropriate tools that lead you to your next one."

3 - GIVE BEFORE YOU ASK

Another strategy that leads to changing your mindset—and this, to me, is very relevant; I am a big supporter of this strategic promotion—is to **give before you ask.**

One of the biggest pitfall examples I see over and over again, presented in the form of an email, will sound like this:

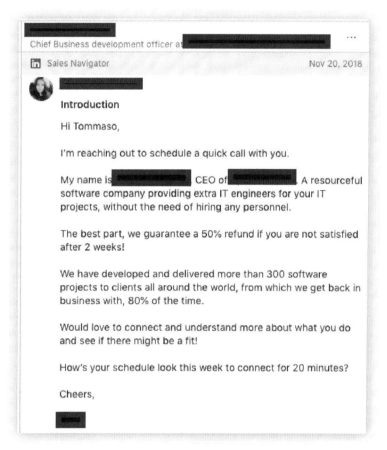

"Hi… I have a great tool. It does it all—you wouldn't think of it—but you will benefit from it, and I want time from you…" or the other option, is they say, "You can also test it."

In other words, the typical email we all receive almost daily is just asking us to either test something or jump on a call with someone we don't know.

Does this seem familiar to you?

Honestly (and unfortunately), **this is what most entrepreneurs do**. Especially with their MVP.

Now, what's wrong with that?

What has surprised me over and over again is how I've had the great pleasure of meeting so many excellent, unique, brilliant brains that are very creative in developing a product that doesn't exist…. Meaning, they put so much energy into a product and making something new, and then it seems that when it gets to the point of bringing this product to market, all the excellence and uniqueness and especially the creativity that this exact person had in developing the product gets lost.

Why?

Because they turn on their plain vanilla mode setting, sending out emails and asking for things the same way everyone else does. This tends not to trigger anyone's curiosity at all.

And guess what?

It is not going to lead to any engagement.

Allow me tell you **why it won't convert:**

The psychology of a persona deciding to take action based on what they have read is triggered by massive curiosity.

Why should somebody give you time, or test something of yours, if they don't know you at all, and have no reason to be curious about you?

So, to contrast this email example: rather than asking for something from your persona right off the bat, you ask yourself **how you can make them curious about your product.**

In order to ask your target audience, influencer or collaborator for something, you have to **give first. You have to bond with them, first.**

This is how I put it to every single startup I advise:

In order to help navigate entrepreneurs I mentor, in this specific **give before you ask tactic**, my main question is, "what is your **value ladder offering**?

What is a **value ladder offering**?

In a value ladder offering, as the word says, you draft up a letter of three, four, maybe five steps. On the top of the ladder, you always find the ultimate achievement you are working towards in your activity, which in many cases is "buy my product". So you write in this ladder, as a step: "buy my product".

Before buying a product, however—especially in enterprise products—you have a trial version of it, which is the previous step before "buy my product". So you write "trial of product" above it.

And before the trial step is the "one-on-one demo", where you get on the phone and demonstrate something. And the goal of this demonstration of your product, in an online conversation, is to **drive curiosity**.

In other words, *this* is actually the moment where you convey enough value in a quality moment: while you are hanging out in a one on one with this specific person.

If you are asking for just a demo in an email, you're not conveying enough.

In the value ladder, your first step as an entrepreneur is **to bond, and not to ask.**

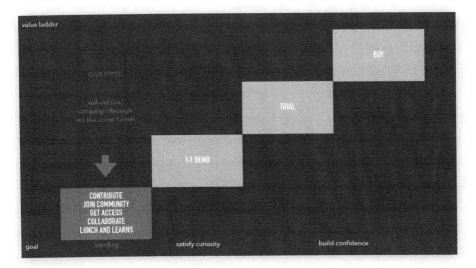

You may now be intrigued on how you bond. Well, you bond by doing activities, which I call **inclusive marketing activities**. Within these inclusive marketing activities, as the word says, is where you include your target persona; where you make your buyer persona a part of your product, rather than just trying to sell it to them.

In other words, you make your target audience part of what you do; you make them *feel* like a part of your brand.

I'll give you a couple of examples of these **inclusive marketing activities**:

You can, for example, say, "Hey, <name>! Come, and let's collaborate on this thing together!" **This one's pretty obvious.**

OR, you can invite them to "join an exclusive community!"

People can start interacting and engaging with your brand before you even get to your product. In other words, you can develop and then invite your target persona to join an existing closed community, where you give your buyer persona the chance to understand your knowledge, your experience and your vision of your brand, before you actually ask them to use your product.

OR another example is....

Rather than sending your persona an offering in the form of a whitepaper download, which is very static as an approach (meaning you send your persona something to download and they have the possibility of doing so), you ask your buyer persona by reaching out to them, in a very selective way (in other words not for everybody, but *in a certain role in a certain industry*, scarcity style) to contribute to an ebook you are writing. And then this ebook is all about the topic of what your product is representing. For instance, the future of VR in your industry. Or Conversion Rate Optimization on Websites from a VP Perspective. So you, instead of just sending something optional to your buyer persona, now create something together with them; with their contribution.

Now, with creating something like this ebook, it's not about the outcome. It's not about having this thing in your hands. **It's about what happens between you and your buyer persona.**

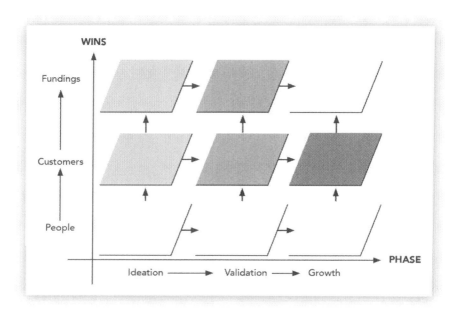

And you know what happens?

You build a relationship. And if you're building a relationship, for those of you who are underestimating it, you are building trust, and trust is the fundament of the persona feeling confident in testing your product, in buying your product, and in becoming a craving fan of your product.

Another example of this is something I call the **Online to Offline Strategy**.

An example is, for instance, rather than approaching your buyer persona through a channel [which, regardless of what it is, will be online ads via social outreach platforms such as Facebook, LinkedIn, email, etc.], you actually take this relationship offline.

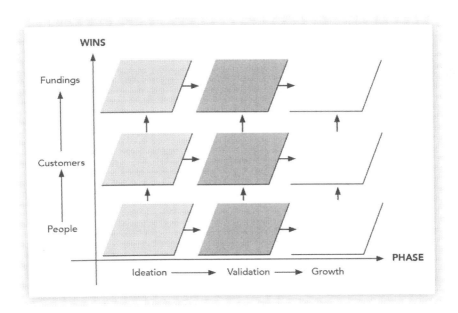

Some of you may be thinking, "What does Tommaso mean by offline?"

Or even perhaps, "Well, if I do go offline, I won't be scalable."

Well, here we are again: **In the beginning, it's not about being scalable.** In the beginning, it's actually about you doing activities that lead to a relationship. Because a relationship gives you access to your buyer persona feeling engaged with your product, rather than you thinking of scaling before doing the first step; before fulfilling the first step of your value ladder offering.

<u>Give first</u>.

Invite them for a for lunch-and-learn! Meet your target audience and your influencers **in person**.

For example, if you are a B2B, you can run lunch-and-learn activities where you take a small budget of a few hundred dollars, and invite a few handfuls of executives to a lunch-and-learn event focused around you, where you talk about your topic.

In this activity, first of all, if nobody is coming, you understand that either your product, or your messaging, or your value proposition are broken—something is broken, so you understand if there is some other issue. But if they show up, you start building your community. And then, a repeatable way of giving before you ask is to repeat this process in multiple cities.

Another version of this activity which creates brand authority and thought leadership [wherein you actually pay forward your knowledge], is hosting a podcast or video e-series. What you do there is start podcasting about your topic in a way similar to what I explained above, or you just start recording and make a weekly appointment to do so! "On Thursdays at 2pm, I go live!"

You can use this as an opportunity to interview your influencers and show them what you do.

At the beginning, with the first interview, you will struggle. At the beginning, with the first video session, it will be strange to you. Perhaps you are not confident in front of the camera. The second time, maybe friends will make fun of you, but… think forward.

After twenty, thirty, forty, sixty episodes that you collect, you have so much power—so much market penetration, so much knowledge that you share, so much good that you've done for the market—that it becomes a snowball effect that comes back, only in positive reaction. And usually, this reaction comes in the form of inbound strategies, with inbound leads that you activate based on the content that has been shared, and shared again.

So, give!

You know what they're going to ask *you* at the end, after a lunch-and-learn or a podcast discussion? They're going to say, "Thank you for taking the time and thinking of me! Now, tell me, *what is it that you do?*"

Aha! So they're curious now!

We want to have incentives, rather than bang our heads against a brick wall asking the world *why* it is so difficult to create traction with collaborators!

Instead of selling yourself, win someone over.

To increase conversion rates, the ask comes after you've provided initial value. **Inclusive activities make your persona feel like a part of your brand.**

An example of this is the tool GrowthHackers.com. Sean Ellis, founder and CEO, has basically coined the term "growth hacking". His tool is amazing in how it allows you to manage multiple growth hacks simultaneously with ease. Growth hacking is always AB testing different campaigns, so you need something that measures and tracks and collaborates with your team members, and this tool does it.

Sean Ellis sent an email out to his influencers and contacts. Take a look to see how he approached his persona:

So what is Sean doing with this email? Is he asking me to test the tool? Is he asking me to buy the tool? Is he asking me to try the tool?

No. He's saying, "This is a growth hacking tool, this is a growth hack *for you*, and *this* is how you use it."

He is **giving**, because he basically says, "I'm bonding, and providing value first."

Provide value first. **Then** start engaging.

Now, let me follow up with SWAAAG, and what I did with the app in reference to this part of this promotional strategy; of giving before you ask.

Remember, my main target group with the SWAAG app was teenagers. And kids, as I said earlier, are tremendously opinionated, and therefore challenging to convert for a new product.

In fact, I would go so far as to say they are within the most challenging target audience to get to, because of how they're less about rationality and facts, and all about the emotions and network effect. If you don't capture them emotionally, they are not coming. If their friends are not there, they are not joining. Period.

Back then, I spent a lot of time thinking about how to grow my user base. At the time, Instagram was the big thing, so I asked myself how I could capture the kids who use Instagram.

I realized that my benefits were:

1) You could use videos, where no one else was at the time.
2) Those videos could have a rating, which isn't an option elsewhere.
3) The user experience was more fun than other platforms, due to the influencer connections I offered.

What I decided to do next is a surprise to me, even to this day. What I figured to do as a test was to create an offline event, along the lines that I described above, called **The SWAAAG Event.**

I invited kids to the event with three pieces of information. Come and:

1) Eat pizza
2) Meet friends
3) Participate in a competition

Notice what I *didn't* mention?

Anything at all about SWAAAG, or the value of the app itself. Rather, with this activity we focused on providing a great offline experience "powered by SWAAAG".

So what happened was, on a Saturday afternoon, fifty kids arrived to this open air location.

And this is how I kicked it off:

I said: "Thanks for coming. *This* is what will happen today…. First, feel free to have a slice of pizza." Then, I said: "Second, Meet your peers."

Then, "Oh, and *by the way*… at the end, you can win a hoodie if you participate in this challenge."

"Oh!!! great!!!" The kids said in chorus, "What's the challenge?"

"The challenge is: **You have to capture and share thrilling moments today, and your peers will rate the video.**"

There. There is my plug. I mean, how subtle can you get?

I'll show you….

"So, wait! What app do we use for the competition?" The teenagers asked me, "Instagram? Vine?"

Another kid was quick to respond, "No way! Instagram doesn't *do* video."

Another shouts questionably, "Vine only does six second videos! Facebook?"

And another says in rapid succession, "Ugh, I *hope* it's not Facebook. Our parents are on Facebook."

I say, "**Glad you asked. Download SWAAAG.**"

BOOM. Mic drop.

Perfect product placement, launched straight to my difficult-to-reach target audience.

We received 3,000 downloads, just from this activity.

And why is this?

Because we **gave first**, aimed to **build a relationship**, and we **created something that they wouldn't expect.**

This, to me, is the *mantra* of that story:

Take your target audience **beyond** what they expect to get from your product.

Your customer is always full of expectation, and this expectation is usually expressed by the benefits you provide.

Now, in order to take them beyond, you have to present something that they are not expecting your tool to provide.

Again, SWAAG was an app, so they expected the video. What did we do? We took them beyond, by doing an offline event.

What is your **minimum expected product** [MEP] (unlike the minimum viable product)?

You, as an entrepreneur, must do activities where you give, and you take your persona beyond. When you do this; when you take them beyond, you create a unique experience.

So take your persona beyond this minimum expected product.

Wherever you surprise your persona, by giving them more than they expect, is where you **hook them.** Brand experience starts when you give your persona something that is unexpected and/or additional.

The experience your persona has with your tool, and with you, is where you find your uniqueness. Offline experiences, especially these days, add a particular value and momentum to your product.

Hey. So. If you practice this, you will rock every single growth hack.

You just have to take them *beyond*...

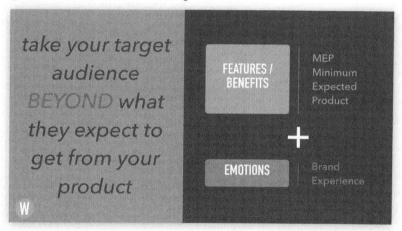

If your tool is a marketplace, people expect you to connect A with B. Why? Because this is what a marketplace does.

If this was a social community app, you know what they would expect? That they can comment on the posts, share media, share their thoughts, and basically craft their own small community.

This is what they expect.

What they *don't* expect is for you to take them beyond and give them emotions. Make them *feel*.

This is where they start bonding with your brand, so this is where you start giving.

The takeaway here: **People don't buy stuff, they buy what stuff does with them. Personally. Emotionally.**

Your *goal* is to create emotion.

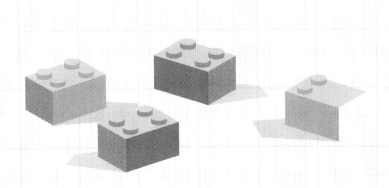

"People Don't Buy Stuff, They Buy What Stuff Does With Them."

#GiveBeforeYouAsk

4 - CONTROLLED PROCRASTINATION

The fourth promotional strategy under the umbrella of **changing your mindset** is the **strategy of controlled procrastination**. For example:

Here is a behavioral tactic that I have learned since moving to Silicon Valley. When I first made the move, I noticed that many peers I tried to meet with who were in startups or raising funds had an urge to meet with me right away to connect and make decisions.

But, on the investor side, I would mostly receive responses like, "Thank you for contacting me, I will be travelling next week, and the following week I am at a conference, and away for three more weeks." Or I would get things like (to make a long story short), "Let's push this discussion back, and connect in the future. Please reach out to me in xxx time."

This, from the perspective of the receiver, created the sustenance, or the need, to crave even more for this specific meeting. But only because you were meeting an investor. However, this theory applies just as well to the relationship between you and your customer.

If you receive an inbound message—regardless if it's through a chat bot, or through an email—and you respond right away, you are signaling that, on the one hand yes you are available, but on the other hand you are not giving the person who has contacted you / the tender the necessary space to mature the thought process.

Why?

Because all of us, as soon as we start interacting, are more trained in our behavior to close something, to win something, to make something happen right away. But this oftentimes is actually working against the acceleration of the win.

And why is this?

From a psychological perspective, if you react after 24 hours but before 48, the person who reached out to you starts craving a response. They want to hear from you during this timeframe.

Meaning, if you reach back right away, it's too much. It's too soon. If you talk to them *after* two days, you lose them because you are not showing importance. But if you just do it the right way, after 24 hours, this becomes the perfect moment to present yourself with something like, "Hey, I've got this on the table. I'm all for you right now."

Often, it's counterintuitive to think that *right away* translates to a faster acceleration of the sale cycle, but again, give space and procrastinate—**proactively procrastinate.**

Meaning, do not lose the lead, but know what you are doing. This can apply, then, to investors, customers, colleagues, and press. Why? Because you are busy, but on top of things, and everybody has their own turn within the 24 hours response time.

Decades later, as I've found myself understanding and living "controlled procrastination", it is a strength rather than a weakness if you are on top of things. Regardless, whether it's a potential new partner, investor, family member, or whatever, things get baked in a better way when you allow them the time they need to mature; the time to *breathe*.

Psychologically, if you don't respond to inquiries right away, you create a suspense towards the recipient, which makes the engagement more valuable.

For instance, if you got an email from a prospect, where you got them to appoint wanting to meet you, don't answer the same day. It signalizes you desperately want this meeting. I know how startups desperately need every meeting, but if you respond 24hrs later, your customer gets impulses of sovereignty—rather than hectic desperation.

And remember, the sum of all the impulses we set when we engage with our prospects and customers is where we define the customer experience.

Speaking needs space.

Listening is of the utmost importance.

It is the foundation of all communication.

So, my advice to you early entrepreneurs is to allow the pie to set in a controlled tactical manner; not to push too hard. We respond within the 24 hours, but not after 48.

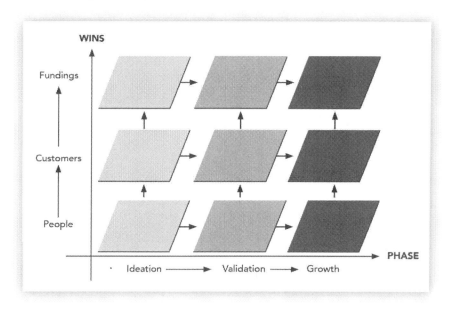

5 - FEAR OF MISSING OUT

I would like to take a moment here to explain the relevance of strategic promotions.

Again, most entrepreneurs just offer something to the market, rather than building a tactic and a promotion around **how they convey** that this product is available to the market, in order to make the persona feel the urge to take advantage **now.**

The Now is what matters most, and what leads you, through applying these strategic promotional strategies, to the most advantageous engagement.

One of the next examples I would like to break down is called **FOMO: The Fear of Missing Out.**

To put this strategy simply: Rather than just offering a product to every member of the target audience, you limit the access, the availability.

You restrict, basically, this offer to either:

1) Make it available in a certain period of time,
2) Make it available to certain roles within a certain period of time,
3) Make it available in a certain geographical location,
4) Make it available to a certain amount of customers, or to
5) Make it available only for the first customers who take action.

Again, the psychology behind FOMO; this Fear of Missing Out, is that, for the human being, when you just offer something, and you simply make something available to them; you are leaving it up to them to decide if and when they wish to respond, or whether they are interested in taking action or not. If you put this under the umbrella of a FOMO strategy, you instead say to them, basically, "Well, you can decide, but within *this* framework."

This leads you into a more structured pipeline approach, because you set the dates, you set the restrictions, and you always have more leverage towards your customer, because you always have a fixed date, or a fixed role, or you have certain boundaries that you impose onto the customer's response.

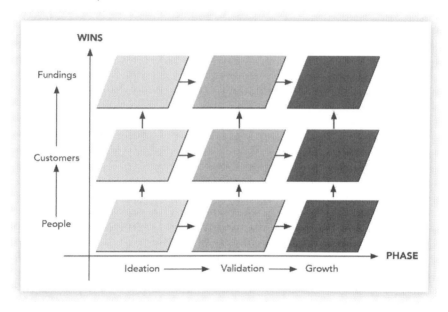

6 – PRESENTING VALUE + STEPPING AWAY

Another high conversion promotional strategy to supercharge your mindset is **to present your value and then step away.**

You can apply this tactic to increase your conversion rates, especially when using traction channels such as email marketing, social media, or personal outreach, for instance on Facebook, Instagram or LinkedIn. [In other words, everywhere you have a one-on-one interaction with your potential persona.]

The goal, usually, when reaching out to a persona, is to make an ask, and accomplish a specific call to action.

For instance, when you describe your product, again in this cited traction channel, you generally end your outreach copy with something like, "When is a good time for you to have a conversation?" Or else, "What do you think about taking a look at our product?"

What you are doing by contacting them in this way is handing the decision-making process over to the recipient. Meaning, you are asking the recipient whether they are interested in taking the meeting, or taking a demo, or whatnot.

So they say either yes or no to it. But it's all up to them, and you're left waiting for them, with nothing to show for your efforts. The balls are all in their court.

Now, with the lean in and step back approach, you present value (meaning to explain what you do), but instead of ending with a fixed call to action, you actually can finish the conversation with something like, "By the way, dismiss if disinterested." Or, "Dismiss if disinterested, but happy to chat otherwise."

What happens, when you complete your outreach on this note, is that the recipient is no longer in a position to decide whether they want what you're offering or not. The ball is no longer in their court.

You are basically saying, in other words, and in a very strict and direct way, "Hey, listen, if you are not interested, I do not care."

So, **now,** this shows you stepping away from the deal as though you could take or leave their interest, and you're no longer saying, "I'm starving, and I'm craving for this meeting."

Guess what?

99.99% are craving for the meeting. Now, you are the 0.01% who basically says, "I don't care if we meet, but this is the value that we will provide if we do."

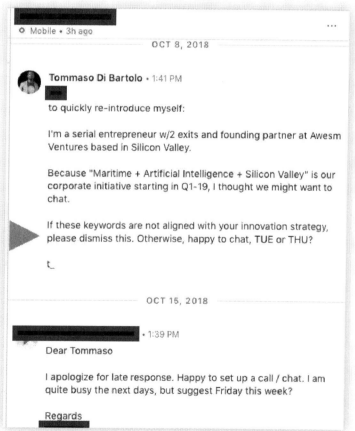

You are showing a unique position, and because of that, the probability of people engaging with you is much higher. They say, "Hey hold on, I don't wanna lose you; I don't want to dismiss this. I actually would like to do something."

So, you are causing exactly the opposite reaction by using this approach, as I was saying in the beginning, where you **increase your conversion rates in a one-on-one outreach**.

7 – PROACTIVE MEETING COORDINATION

I have learned, over the past two decades of approaching different markets, how to expedite the phase between an email conversation and a one-on-one meeting.

What do I mean by this?

In many cases, when we start messaging back and forth on any of the online platforms or similar mediums with our prospects, we tend to be of service, and respond to their questions, or to requests such as, "Hey, can you send me a one-pager of this, or a video of this, so I can get a sense of it?"

What 99% of entrepreneurs do, is fulfil this request. Every time. They send them the one-pager. They send them the video.

And then the hustle begins.

You get back to them a day or two later asking, "Hey, did you take a look at the one-pager I sent you?"

And you get no response for one, two, maybe three days. And then, eventually, you maybe do get a response, saying, "Hey, sorry, I was busy, and haven't gotten to it yet."

And so, you keep on pushing the connection back in your pipeline, further and further. And the days go by, the weeks go by, and (oftentimes, unfortunately), the prospect gets colder, and colder, until you lose them from your pipeline completely.

Wouldn't it be cool if you could actually increase the momentum where the customer has expressed interest, and convert them into a scheduled and qualified meeting?

Allow me to present you with the **proactive meeting coordination**.

In the proactive meeting coordination, what you do (to use the example I gave you above) is, while you are talking and delivering information, you do not end by simply sending them something they have requested.

Yes, you send out an invite, a one-pager, a video, or whatever it is they have requested, but you also add, "P.S. I'll be sending you, also, an invite to block a slot in our calendars for a meeting on Tuesday at 9am, and we will take the coordination of it from there."

What does this cause?

It causes you to proactively and, actually, help the recipient to make the decision to move forward on your deal. You force them to choose **now** whether they wish to follow through or not.

And guess what? It is better for them to come back and cancel the meeting in a short period of time, rather than for you to sit hoping, still after three weeks, that you will get the meeting.

In this approach, your pipeline will be cleaner; it will be way more real, leaving you time to concentrate on other things. The other side effect that's beneficial to the receiver is, now all of a sudden, you've helped them make the decision of, "Yes, we *will* do a meeting!"

This also limits the back and forth between all the assistants, because you just sent him or her a direct invite! So for this, **out of ten invites, you usually will convert 7-8 meetings.**

Obviously, make sure that, in this meeting, you are qualifying the person you're talking to. Because you could end up wasting a lot of your time setting up meetings with this strategy, but with the wrong people.

So make sure that you qualify the right persona. And then present the meeting.

8 – MEETING TO MEETING TO WIN

Along the lines of the strategy of Proactive Meeting Coordination, where you send out a meeting, the **Meet to Meet to Win** allows entrepreneurs to guide their persona to the win.

Imagine! You are in a situation where you have just demonstrated, online, the product you're serving your customer. Usually, at the end of most demos like these, you end up on a **potential next task**.

So what's the potential next task? What are the major outcomes here?

They may say, "Send me something". Or they say, "Send me a proposal", or, "I would like to test it" (in an ideal situation).

In any case, what you are doing here is getting into the next phase of the sales cycle.

Question is, how are you entering this phase?

Are you entering the phase by saying, "Yes, I will send you something"?

If you are, generally what happens next is, the persona will not be available. The proposal has not been read. The video was not clear to a colleague. "We have not gotten there."

So, basically, there are many reasons why they are delayed and delayed and delayed.

Or, you can avoid this situation altogether, and target your outreach with the following strategy:

"Dear customers / potential prospects, I obviously will send to you, at the end of this conversation, as requested, what we have agreed upon."

This could be the proposal. This could be the PDF. This could be the video.

"But I also know, dear prospect, that you are very busy in your activity. And the documents and video, next to your daily job, are actually more of an effort to go through. So what I would like to offer to you here, and what I have a lot of experience in, is to take a look at the calendar now, and to schedule another twenty to thirty minute call, where I can walk you through the highlights of the proposal, video, or relevant collateral I've sent to you."

By the way, what has been working very well in the past is to also invite other colleagues. In other words, you don't have to evangelize, and repeat and repeat the process we just went through.

You can simply say, "Hey, I made something cool. We have a thirty minute call scheduled *here*. I would like you to join, and allow me to put in the effort to evangelize all the others.

Now, dear prospect / dear persona, is it better for you to talk on Tuesday next week at 6pm, or do you prefer Wednesday at 3pm?"

So, what happens here is you actually understand the problem, and the challenge, and the efforts of your potential buyer persona. And because you understand it, you go the next step, and you go from meeting to meeting.

When I say "from meeting to meeting", and I finalize actually on the win, what I say is **every single time you talk with your potential prospect, who becomes a marketing qualified prospect, who becomes a sales qualified prospect, you never end communication without scheduling a meeting.**

The statistics show, and the experiences have proven, that if somebody tells you at the end of the conversation, "Well, <name>, I'm not sure. Let me think about it." Meaning, pushing back the next meeting, and not scheduling the next meeting to review the document; to review the proposal, you can be almost at 90% confidence that this will not close.

But if the person says, "Yes, this sounds great", then you have a qualified, tangible pipeline, and you can walk them from meeting to meeting, to the actual win.

This will give you confidence as an individual, confidence as an employee, or will position you toward your investor as somebody who, when you say you have something in your pipeline, can close it in good time, because you guide the persona the whole way, and nothing occurs out of coincidence.

Because I like to dance, I often compare this idea to dancing to latino music. Traditionally, when you dance to latino music, you, as a man, guide the woman. **You never lose touch with the woman.**

Why?

Because you are guiding them. And the person on the other side is dancing with you because you fit like a glove. So, you guide, and you have a beautiful, gorgeous, rhythmic appearance.

You have fun, you bond, and you both win.

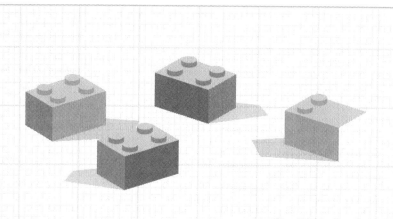

> "Every Single Time You Talk With Your Prospect, Your Minimum Outcome is a Scheduled Next Meeting."

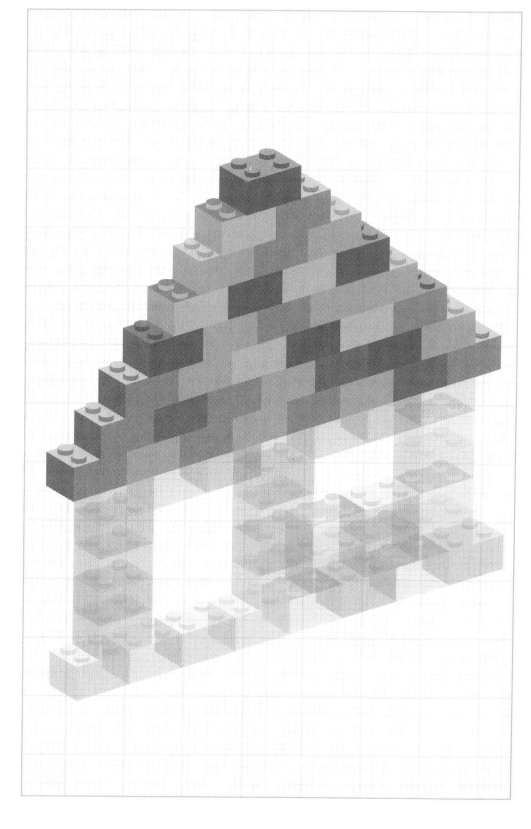

PILLAR TREE

EXECUTING COHERENTLY: DISCOVER THE RIGHT TOOLS

Growth Hacking is the grease between the gears of your Go-To-Market Strategy.

In order to change gears smoothly within your GTM, a good growth hack is dependent on innovative tools.

1 – STOP SPRAYING + PRAYING

This is where you begin to execute.

Most of the startups I meet through innovation initiatives, whether those be mentorship programs, pitch events or being and advisory board member to their ventures, come with the intention to run primarily a *one-step* activity, rather than a plan on how to create a consistent Go-To-Market funnel—aka a series of activities that are linked to each other with the result of a "win".

Stop. No more random, isolated, stand-alone activities. Meaning, if you're just planning a Facebook ad to increase clicks, consider how you can actually activate this person who took action. Or, if you add a link in your Instagram bio to a specific website, consider how can you convert the visitor into a prospect. Or… well, you get what I mean with one standalone activity.

Instead of standalone activities, understand that you have to have a **coherent activity plan**, including what the call to action is, how it triggers an activity to a website or app, where you lead them from there, etc. You have to be aware that every funnel is based upon three, four, five different steps that define your persona's journey.

As such, for every single funnel stage, you need to have a call-to-action and a potential outcome that you are aiming to achieve. And with that, you **use tools that are optimized for each specific funnel stage**.

To create awareness, and ultimately to build trust, one needs four to eight touchpoints in order to make the human being interact. So, if you only fulfil one activity, like sending out an email, don't wonder when you have a minimum response rate. [Especially since email sucks nowadays.]

Ultimately, you build this journey that navigates your persona step by step through to engagement.

Yes. You can, and **tools are here to help you**.

The interesting thing about discovering a tool in today's world is that it can actually lead you towards a go-to-market strategy that was previously not possible to be considered.

What does this mean?

This means I can step back from active marketing, and allow the tool to show me the strategy.

If you design your strategy first, then you've already defined what you're going to use. Whereas, in growth hacking, **you discover the tools first, and the tools give you the strategy.**

Chrome Web Store, Phantom Buster, ProductHunt, Siftery has a plethora of apps that help you growth hack.

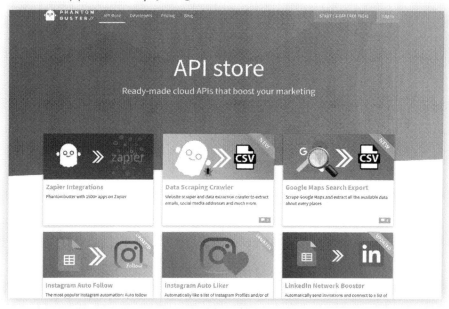

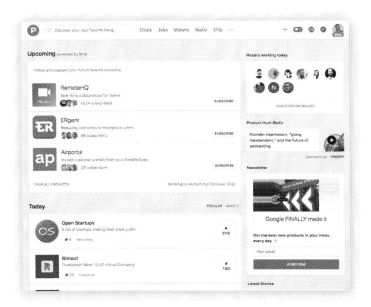

Most of the tools you'll find are things you have seen already, so you will have to put in the effort to test a lot of them at first, to see which ones work best for you and your needs.

But that's the beauty, right?

Finding the uncluttered channel.... Especially putting in the effort that saves you the dollars and team members you may not currently have. Bridge the gap to the uncluttered channel by testing and finding the right tools for your needs.

Pitfall number one here, with most startups, is how they do a little bit here, and a little bit there… scattering their efforts.

REMEMBER: You have to stop just spraying your efforts, and praying that something sticks.

Okay? So this is **not** how you approach your go-to-market.

What you *do* need is a funnel.

"Oh, yes that's *obvious*."

"Great! If it's so obvious, why didn't you do it?"

2 - THE G-AARRR FUNNEL: ONE STAGE AT A TIME

When talking about funnel in Go-To-Market / Growth Hacking often, one funnel that comes to mind is the AARRR Funnel, most frequently known for its inventor Accelerator 500 Startup, in Silicon Valley. It's a Simple way to break down the customer journey into five phases.

Each of these bars represents one of the phases in how you bring your product to market, and for each of these phases, you can attach a tactic and tool.

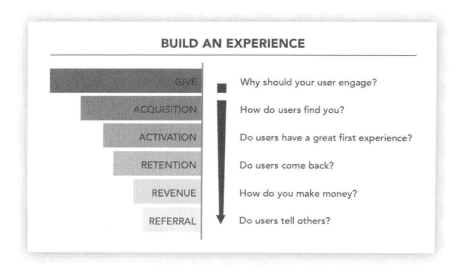

So, I've added a first step before any other—GIVE—to maximize funnel benefits. It's really about **what you put into the funnel** that counts.

Step Number One: GIVE.

While we expand upon the chapter *Give Before You Ask*, here are a couple more examples on how to come up with your giving strategy for your funnel.

"How can I **give**, Tommaso? How can I *come up with something*? **What** should I give?"

I have very simple metrics, which I was able to configure once I understood what I was doing:

So here's what you do:

Let's say you have a health app. In order to **take the user beyond,** you have to offer activities that are also about health, yet may not necessarily be attached to your app.

For instance, you can form an offline gym group, or invite people to run a 5K in a public park on a certain date. The event has to do with health, yet isn't the app; the event is powered by the app, yet **I am the one who takes them beyond**.

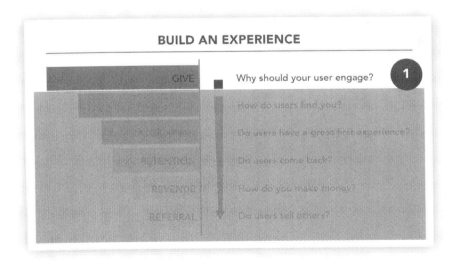

And why would you do this?

Because your target audience does not expect you to. And because of this "over-delivery", you will start bonding with them.

This is especially important early on, as you need fans to support your endeavor. You need people rooting for you, waiting and salivating for what you have to offer next.

Typical pitfalls of a giving strategy are for instance:

- Extending a free trial from 7 to 14 days
- Giving a freemium license

Why? Because in a giving strategy it is about creating an "experience" which is not "the product" but something along the lines of the product. Meet your audience offline and create moments they can't forget!

Step Number Two: ACQUISITION.

Acquisition stands for where to acquire your buyer persona. Understanding where they hang out; where they spend their time is fundamental for you to know where to "fish" for their curiosities.

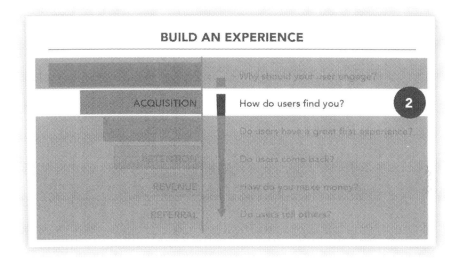

One of the current hacks which has led many portfolio startups of ours to growing results, primarily in the B2B space, is the following, called the **LinkedIn Acquisition Strategy:**

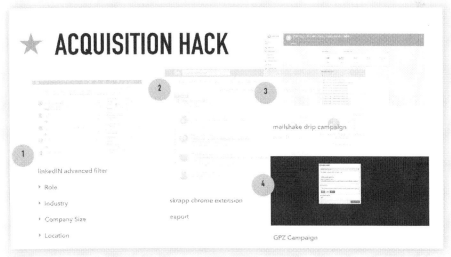

First, subscribe to the LinkedIn Sales Navigator, which provides you with unlimited search results and an advanced search option.

Remember though, that before you invest dollars in this tool, you need to have your bullet loaded and ready to shoot.

With that I mean, as in Pillars One and Two, how we expanded upon the Communication and the Strategic Promotion. Which, if you don't understand by now, and yet you start using the tools, you cannot expect atypical conversion rates, because you're missing the juice of the fruit for how these specific tools can even help to increase your conversion rates.

One of the biggest pitfalls is in how startups focus right away on tools. They focus on tools, but actually, it is **the words you say**, and **how you utilize your promotional strategies**, that expedites the usefulness of the tools. You need **communication** and **promotional strategies** under your belt before you use any tools.

To begin with, you start creating an event filter to narrow down the buyer persona. For example, you could search for someone in the role of Director of Customer Care, in the Manufacturer industry, located in San Francisco, working in a company sized between 100 and 500 employees.

Why is this important?

Because I take this filtered result, and combine it with the targeted copy for my outreach.

The copy could be something like, "Hey <name>, we've run an activity for Director of Customer Care in the Manufacturer Industry, of a company size between 100-500, located in San Francisco, and I thought you might want to chat. What's a good time on Tuesday or Wednesday for a quick intro call? Dismiss if disinterested."

Obviously, the activity I'm mentioning here needs to be enriched, without adding too much, while making it clear what the activity direction might be. In many cases, because we work in text, you can say something like, "We run an innovation activity".

So once I have the filter set, I use tools that put the entire LinkedIn activity on steroids. One of the tools I like working with is, for instance, GPZ for LinkedIn or, the even more useful LinkedHelper.

An activity I map out with these tools is comprised of the following steps:

1) Follow your target audience. With this activity, the persona gets the message that you have followed them, and obviously you want to make sure that your LinkedIn is appealing enough for this person to desire following you back. In fact, 5-20% do so. Congratulations on your first touchpoint!

2) Send a content request (not an inmail, signaling you're spamming), in which you are very straightforward and valuable at the same time in what you are asking. Ideally with this second step, you do not ask anything yet, in order to increase the top of the pipeline acceptance rate. In other words, if you ask to meet right now, versus if you just want to connect for future synergy, the ones aiming for future synergy will have a higher acceptance rate.

3) Now, you leverage the feature to endorse your persona. The psychology behind this is that everybody likes to get an endorsement, regardless of whether you know the investor personally or not, so you show appreciation for this person, and one more time, congratulations on your touchpoint!

4) What I do, and suggest a portfolio company of ours whose needs parallel to this activity to do is to, as soon as you have a person connected with you, publish three to five daily, **relevant** posts on your LinkedIn feed. Remember when we say relevant, it must add value to the person who has recently connected with you. As a result of this, you now have a vali-

dated content machine that increases awareness due to multiple touchpoints accessed through your feed. In order to automate this process, you can use Quuu.com in combination with Buffer.com.

5) Now, it's time to go for the **ask**. You can go either with a soft ask or with a hard ask. With a soft ask, I refer to an inclusive market strategy, or with the hard ask, I ask for a meeting. The biggest pitfall here is people don't **integrate this ask** into a promotional strategy. Again, if you tell me, "Tommaso, do you want to meet?" This is not leading to huge conversion rates, versus if you say, "Tommaso, only three people in San Francisco are invited… Dismiss if you are disinterested." Again, it's all about how you offer the thing, not the fact that you offer what you are doing. The good news about the ask is it doesn't need to be done manually, but you can use again the tools I am referring to as an automated activity to connect all of your most recent contacts. Meaning, it starts sending out the message to your most recently accepted contact requests.

6) As a result of this activity, you will have three main possible results: 1. not responding, 2. asking for more info, or 3. agreeing on the ask, where obviously you then start prioritizing the most interested and interesting prospects amongst them.

Conversion rates, over the past three years, between contact request and request acceptance, have been at a minimum of 10-35%.

And then, after this, you can start to *elegantly* get in contact with them directly in one of two ways:

1) Through LinkedIn directly by using GPZ, another great tool
2) By putting it in a drip campaign.

Step Number Three: ACTIVATION.

Activation is what you want your target audience to undertake when in touch with your product. In other words, what you want your visitor *to do* in order to become a lead.

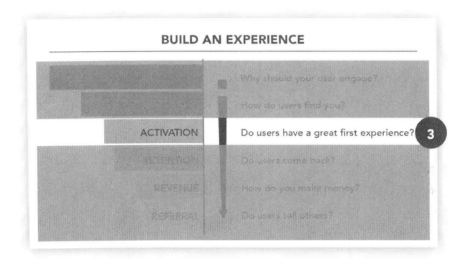

Imagine you drove traffic to your website by leveraging an acquisition strategy as previously discussed. What are some tools that can help you convert your prospect into a marketing qualified lead?

A timely tactic of 2019 is to embed a bot onto your website or tool. What the market is primarily still doing on websites is using forms, sign-ups or offering downloads in order to engage with the prospect. But this is a poor user experience. It's too old style.

A bot is a widget that emulates a human being engaging on the website with the visitor. Let me expand on what I mean by emulation. Emulation is a personalized way of communicating based on who the person is and what they are looking at, while at the same time using an almost urban style to create empathy in the conversation.

The bot is capable of asking a series of interrelated questions that can be either hard-coated, or that the AI will be capable of phrasing on it's own. The result of it is that your marketing-qualified lead has fun engaging with your brand, which will increase the probability of the persona deciding on a call-to-action that has been offered. Such as, "Can I call you back?" or, "Can I send you an email or a text message?"

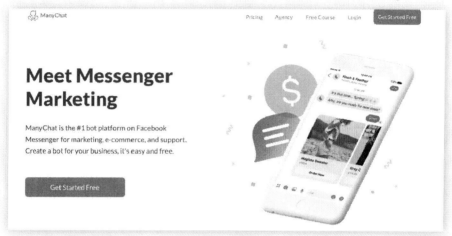

In this way, your sales and marketing can spend time with those leads that are more highly qualified, unlike those sourced from traditional forms or emails.

Some of the most known B2B bots on the market are those from Drift and Intercom. Or also, the most recently released product from HubSpot. Or if you want to connect your visitors with your Facebook activities, you might want to use Manychat.

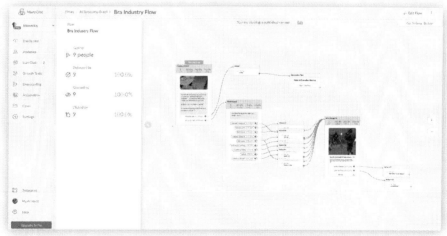

If you now combine these tools with the right promotional strategy, such as the scarcity strategy, it will maximize your visitor-to-lead conversion. "Hey, nice to chat with you… we only have three spots available in New York City" (the tools allow you to configure the visitor's geo-location).

Obviously, if your website also visualizes the statement of a certain requirement to join, or to access your tool in combination with the bot's communication talent, you have a pretty round activation hack.

Visual Trigger

+

Strategic Promotion

+

Communication Automation

Step Number Four: RETENTION.

Retention is when you have prospects or customers, and the question becomes, "How can I make sure they come back?"

Retention is within the most important KPI for any product. The retention rate is the indicator for the level of value that any product is providing to their target audience. Meaning, if the retention rate is low (aka people are not using the app anymore or are not logging into your tool or using it), then you may have huge activation numbers, yes, but they have no worth when the retention rate is low.

Let me expand even more on the definition of retention, because this is a make-it-or-break-it step to your funnel. When asking yourself what your retention rate is, the answer doesn't actually mean anything unless the main usability feature of your tool has been specified.

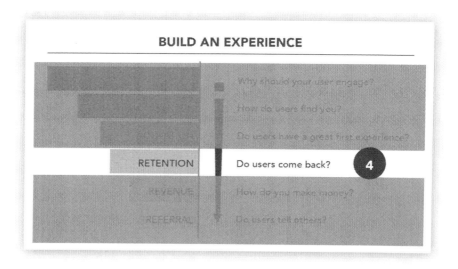

Retention can refer to how many people have opened the app, but has no value if we don't know what the user has actually done on the app.

As an entrepreneur, what you would like to achieve with your product is, when the user comes back to the app, that they contribute to, or operate within your tool, so that it starts to generate more and more value the more often they use it.

For instance, if I sign up on a new CRM [Customer Relationship Management], but I don't grow the contact pool, and have an ongoing communication with them, the probability of leaving this CRM is pretty high still, because the value of the interaction is low.

Based on this fact, when building a hack specifically aimed at retention, it would benefit you to define the success of it by the prospects engaging with your core functionality.

One of the strategies that leads to such an engagement is called **Deep-Linking.**

There are a variety of deep-linking apps on the market. Certainly, Branch.io is one of the most renowned, which allows you to interact with your prospects in a relevant manner across devices, channels and platforms.

Branch.io
Deep link your offer to increase conversions

Bluejeans
Facebook LIVE with multiple parties to create a great experience

To give you an example based on Airbnb, imagine there is a huge event going on in San Francisco on the Peninsula, and therefore, you can deduce that Airbnb's users will be headed to the app, to check out places between Burlingame and Palo Alto.

A decision to rent a place, through, takes multiple attempts because the visitor considers and looks into multiple platforms before deciding to take action. Meaning, unless the visitor has already been to that specific hotel or location, they most likely won't book the first place they look at.

If you don't use deep linking tools within the Airbnb app, the persona will receive an email, in which, if they click on the banner, ad or link, are taken to the main page of the app. AKA not an individualized location based on certain behavior, as would be most beneficial to the visitor.

If the email they receive is deep linked, not only is the email showing the visitor a specific location, such as Burlingame, Redwood City, San Mateo or Palo Alto, but it also takes them directly to the final offering (i.e., the persona's point of interest), thus making the outreach personally relevant to the persona, which increases the probability for them to swipe their credit card.

Deep linking tools are effective because of how they understand the circumstances the person is in, and help them to feel motivated to come back again, as a result.

Retention is increasing the motivation for your persona to return by addressing their needs.

Another cool hack to encourage your prospect to return to your offering (in this case, we assume that your buyer persona has not become a customer yet), is the **Retargeting Strategy.**

Retargeting helps you keep your brand in front of the prospects who haven't yet become customers. While there are a bunch of retargeting tools on the market, the following hack is simple and does not require a standalone retargeting software.

This, by the way, can be an expansion on the **LinkedIn Acquisition Strategy** as described above:

1) Export all your LinkedIn network email addresses (Google how).

2) Import all the email addresses into FaceBook and use a targeted audience when activating a campaign (Google how).

3) The campaign is ideally showing a video testimonial and the call to action allows the prospect to download something of value.

What happens here is that you are catching the attention of your business contacts on a channel that is not equal to the original channel you have been communicating through (aka LinkedIn or email).

60-70% of all exported email addresses on LinkedIn usually match the same email addresses on Facebook, and therefore you will be top-of-mind over and over again in a retargeted manner. Simple. Effective. And low-budget.

Step Number Five: REVENUE.

The question I like to ask when it comes to Revenue is, "How can you create a journey for your buyer persona to become attracted to sign up for your services?"

This is basically the entire picture behind "R" which stands for revenue.

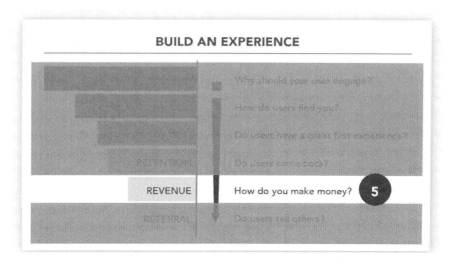

To make it more tangible, let me give you the example of a software-as-service business or product, which in the B2B space, is provided for a test in a trial period. Trials are, actually, very delicate and important things that occur before the decision-making moment.

The prospect is in their decision-making process, asking themselves, "Do I want to become a customer after the trial? Yes or no?"

So, in other words, of course your product must do what you say it does, and must deliver value, but if you provide a great experience during the trial—during the initial phase—the probability increases for them to convert and become a customer.

Now, how do we define experience? Let me walk you through such an experience, by introducing the tool Autopilot.

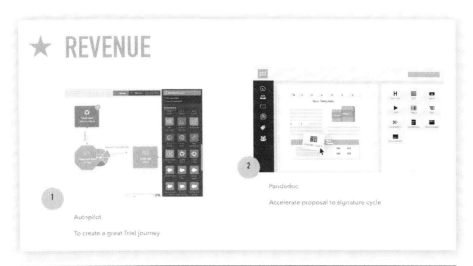

1. Autopilot — To create a great Trial journey
2. Pandadoc — Accelerate proposal to signature cycle

Using this tool, you can configure an email journey directly related to the level of engagement that your user is into. So in other words, it understands what action the user is taking on the tool, and based upon that, triggers emails to guide the user to expand and dive deeper into the tool. Plus, it provides an amazing experience in the process.

Let's say I sign up, but only visit the dashboard, and have not created anything within the tool. The autopilot recognizes this missing activity, and sends me an email along the lines of, "Hey, this is step one, step two, step three for how to create content."

How does this convert into revenue?

Well, many products have a premium product to attract potential customers, and lead them to a premium feature that needs to be activated by committing them to sign up. That's how a tool like this comes in handy.

Another tool I enjoy using is called Pandadoc. Pandadoc expedites the process from the proposal phase to the actual signature. And who doesn't want to expedite that process?!?

So, when you do enterprise business, and you are at the stage where you send your potential new customer a proposal, it's all about reading terms and conditions, checking pricing, making sure the customer bundles products together, and providing signatures through multiple stakeholders.

This is often a very lengthy, nerve-wracking process that requires a bunch of back and forth to update negotiated terms and get, literally, everyone on the same page. Meaning, this process is broken. There exists the need for a tool to make it fun and simple to complete these transactions.

Always remember, every single touchpoint with your prospects and customers must represent a pleasant journey.

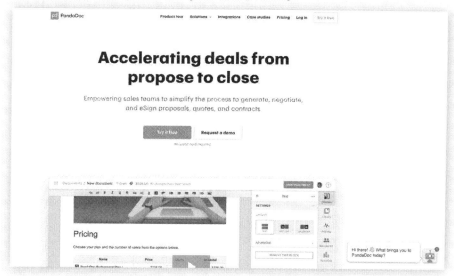

This is where Pandadoc comes into play, and how we advise startups to leverage that:

1) Choose your proposal template and add your corporate identity.

2) Create a video, ideally from the founders of the company, to thank the viewer for their interest, and to showcase the founders as available. Allow me to expand upon the importance of this step: Besides a startup offering a product, we cannot forget that business is conducted between people. And we cannot underestimate the importance of the relationship between a customer and the C level. Obviously, there is a challenge of scalability, therefore a video for this very specific stage makes the CEO available to the customer and signalizes a willingness to collaborate, a humbleness of authenticity, and it differentiates the company from what 99% of others are doing. Aka sending plain PDFs.

3) Create a pricing table with different options from which the prospect can choose. Present a starter package, a professional package, and an enterprise package, with individual features and different pricings per product.

4) Lastly, add a signature field and assign roles for whomever is responsible for signing the document.

By doing this, expect to reach 50% higher value per deal, 30% higher close rate, 50% less microtasks, and 100% accuracy and compliance.

Step Number Six: REFERRAL.

The final part of the funnel.

What is referral?

Basically, when your persona loves so much what you do, that they make the decision to share the details of their pleasant experience with others, and as a consequence invite them to join in, too.

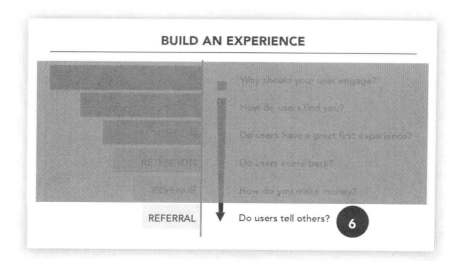

Before moving onto the hack itself, let's make sure that we are on the same page with where the **referral ask is embodied within the customer journey.**

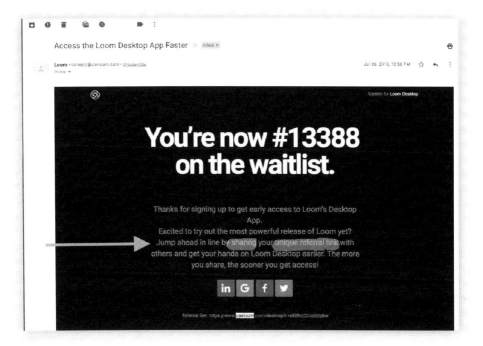

Who has been there, where we download a new app and the first thing it asks you, in the signup process, is if you wish to connect your address book to invite friends. This is a super no-go for the customer journey stage we are in.

Why?

Because the user has just downloaded the tool, and does not know at all the value this tool is providing to them as a user; therefore, why should this new user be motivated to share and invite others if it has zero emotion to it. Meaning, never ask your persona to refer you to another person before an entire journey cycle has been completed.

A couple of examples here:

If you are an app that helps users save money, you make the referral, or call-to-action, visible in every moment where the user actually saves dollars. Once your app has performed as you promised it would comes the moment for *the ask* to come in.

Second, if you are a tool that allows the user to access third-party assets (such as Airbnb, Uber, Lyft, or Lime), ask for the referral when the customer has successfully completed its usage.

You get the picture. **Value first, then ask.**

Again, here are a couple of tactics and tools to support the process of referral. Let me break down tools such as Kickofflabs and Viral-loops.com.

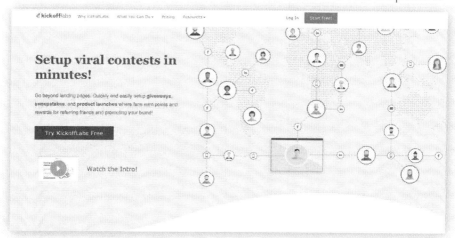

The beauty of these tools is in how they allow us to create a viral contest, including leaderboards, without coding skills. A viral contest is a campaign where you have a giveaway ladder. Meaning, the more customers who have been referred, the more valuable the gift that your customer receives becomes to them.

You ask for a referral, once you deliver, and offer a gift in return.

These tools give you the ability to generate a unique link per person, where they can forward and share on all social media pages. This link also tracks who the referral came through, so they start trending on a leaderboard.

This is fun and simple, and it triggers people to take action, because they are going to be rewarded!

3 – BUILD AN EXPERIENCE

"BUILD IP INTO YOUR GO-TO-MARKET"

Entrepreneurs in startups spend a lot of time and energy building, testing and adjusting products that eventually change the world. During this process, an enormous amount of creativity is involved in building something that doesn't exist today, but might be in all hands tomorrow.

Unfortunately, when it comes time to take this product to market, all of a sudden the brain goes blue screen, the entrepreneurial creativity is lost in translation, and many startup teams approach this fundamental activity without developing the same original thoughts they were using while building the product.

It's almost like saying, on the product side, "I can go nuts", because the majority of the process is more pointed towards spending 90% of the time with the people you know, aka your team. Meaning, there is no situation for fear, or being hesitant, as we are all one big family, and entrepreneurs feel good that they are in a comfort zone.

On the other side, when considering GTM things, the majority of entrepreneurs are taken by the fear of mass rejection from people they don't know, but whom are needed to become their customers. This activity takes massive action to get out of the comfort zone. And because fears primarily limit the human being from executing freely, startup teams want to "play on the safe side"—cannot go nuts—and opt for tactics and tools that everybody else is using to approach the market.

Plain vanilla. Me-too tactics. Poor creativity.

I cannot stress it enough, to summarize: Entrepreneurs: put in the effort to **build your intellectual property equally into your go-to-market**.

"The IP Within the GTM Lies in the Creativity of the Innovator's Execution"

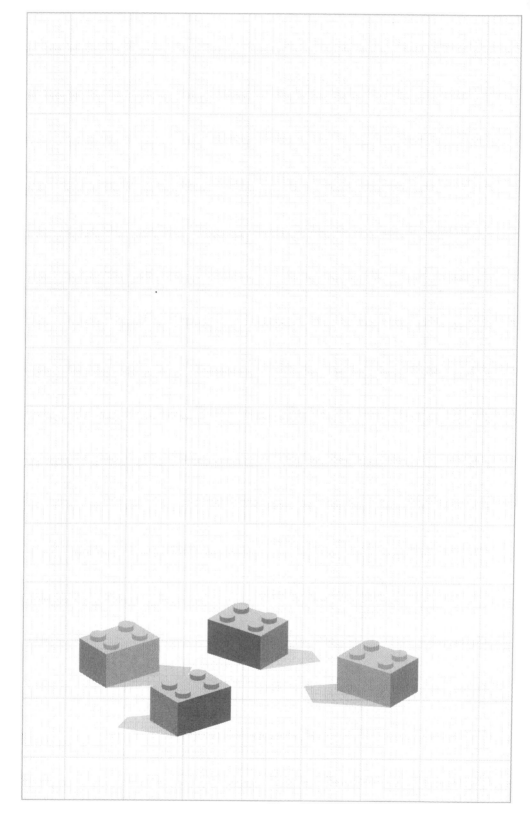

CONCLUSION
IMPLEMENTATION

So, here I'm going to delve into a couple of takeaways I'd love for you to associate with Creative Traction Methodology.

Yes, there's all these guys telling you to curate all these tools that will create magic in your startup….

Sure, there's this idea that the tools make the difference, and are the driving force of growth hacking….

Really though, using these tools is like driving a race car. If you don't have a driver who has been going through years of training, and who understands the circumstances of a racing track, the probability is high that you will wreck the car.

In other words, tools are just the subset of growth hacking.

So really, growth hacking is all about the combination of three ingredients:

Communication. One, every single word counts. Develop the skills to convey things in a unique way.

Promotional Strategies. Two, don't just try to sell a product, but build promotional strategies that make your target audience feel privileged to have access to it.

Executing Coherently. Three, plumb together tools that others are not using to create a timely experience with the highest possible conversion rates.

Think of this picture: with growth hacking, you're building a house.

Question one is to ask: What is your foundation like?

The foundation you lay down before you build your house is based upon **Communication**. It all comes back to the ability of selecting trigger words that cause a reaction. How clearly are you conveying the value of your proposition?

Honestly, even if we had stopped the book after that chapter [The Nuances of Communication], you would still benefit 65% of what growth hacking does.

In fact, feel free to flip back to that section and have a second perspective, now that you understand the three pillars of **CTM**!

Question number two, How many columns are you building your house structure upon?

The second pillar is the strategy of how you build **Strategic Promotions** that make it appealing for your buyer persona to take immediate action. The difference between communication and strategic promotion is that, in communication, you focus on what it is you solve and for whom, while on the side of strategic promotion, you **package the "requirements"** for your customer to get access to your product.

The primary goal here is to leverage upon the emotions that certain strategies are triggering.

Question number three: What's your roof made of?

Finally, you can put the roof on your house, and select tools and channels to use.

The more unique tools you can find that provide a better experience for user interaction [after the above-mentioned has been fulfilled], then the probability of your persona engaging with your product is much higher.

To finalize this anecdote of growth hacking with building a house, as a constructor, you know that you don't start with the roof first.

And lastly, creativity is what lives within the house. **Your creativity.** Your house is a place where you defer judgement, get encouraged by wild ideas, get inspired by third-party sources, and put no limits on how many creative, remarkable user journeys you envision your target audience to undertake.

Stop thinking features. **Start providing experiences.**

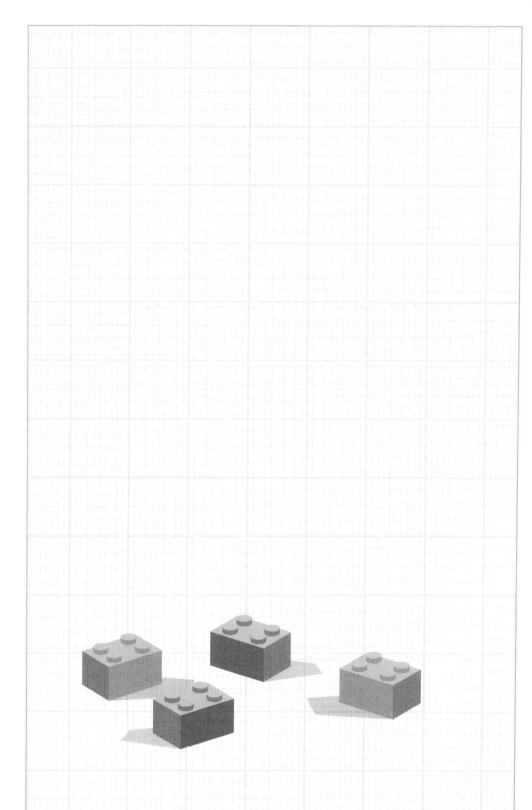

BONUS

HACKS

Below please find useful references: **Tools, Service Providers**, and **Growth Hacking Agencies**, which prove useful in any startup venture.

As we are reading this version of the book, we realize that this list of hacks becomes static. Today, the hacks are appealing, but quickly, they expire... and when they do, you can follow this link to see the updated, curated list of hacks, tools and tactics:

http://Tools-GAARRR.creative-traction.com

Tools + Service Providers

Below is the list of tools and service providers referenced throughout the book, including page numbers, but I have over 400 tools curated, which you can access with the abovementioned link.

Ken Singer | Ken Singer is a serial entrepreneur, technology executive, university lecturer, and director/advisor to numerous startups in the US and Europe. A 15-year veteran of the mobile industry (enterprise software and digital advertising), he has founded or co-founded five companies in the mobility space. Ken's experience spans all forms of mobile technology from mobile video advertising to downloadable mobile apps; from Bluetooth to HTML5, GPS, SMS, IVR, NFC and he has served as a guinea pig for virtually every other acronym in the industry | PG 9

Salesforce | Allows you to integrate every part of your company that interacts with customers onto one platform. | PG 28

Quokka.io | Allows you to provide a retargeting pixel for email or facebook so none of your followers or clients miss your emails or messages. | PG 37

Pixelme | Powers your digital marketing attribution by shortening your links and retargeting pixels. | PG 37

Fiverr | Allows you to hire freelancers on demand, by outsourcing jobs and everyday tasks. | PG 47

Upwork | Allows you to hire freelancers to help you complete your projects through outsourcing. | PG 47

LinkedIn | A business and employment-oriented service that operates via websites and mobile apps, mainly used for professional networking, including employers posting jobs and job seekers posting their CVs. | PG 34, 37, 47, 69, 97, 111, 131, 132, 133, 134, 141

GPZ for LinkedIn | This Linkedin marketing automation software allows online marketers, startup businesses and entrepreneurs to search and find prospects in order to either build a large network of potential customers or strengthen an email list. | PG 47, 133

LinkedHelper | A LinkedIn automation tool, aka bot, which allows you to complete tasks such as auto-endorsing, automatic connection requests, LinkedIn profiles export, bulk-messaging, and group inviting. | PG 47, 133

Facebook | A social media platform which allows you to connect with friends, family and other people you know; share photos and videos, send messages and get updates. | PG 69, 76, 82, 84, 85, 97, 102, 111, 125, 136, 141, 155

Adwords | Google Ads (previously Google AdWords effective July 24, 2018) is an online advertising platform developed by Google, where advertisers pay to display brief advertisements, service offerings, product listings, video content and generate mobile application installs within the Google ad network to web users. | PG 69

Snapchat | A multimedia messaging app, used globally and focused on sharing the moment, in the moment by allowing users to share pictures and messages which are only available for a short time before they become inaccessible to users. | PG 76

Instagram | A photo and video-sharing social networking service owned by Facebook, Inc. | PG 76, 101, 102, 111, 125

YouTube | An American video-sharing website that allows you to share your videos with friends, family, and the world. | PG 76

Vine | A short-form video hosting service where users share six-second-long looping video clips. | PG 76, 102

Google | An American multinational technology company specializing in Internet-related services and products, most famous for their search engine and email tools. | PG 78, 141

Dropbox | A file-hosting service company headquartered in San Francisco, CA, that offers cloud storage, file synchronization, personal cloud, and client software. | PG 83

ProductHunt | A website that lets users share and discover new products; where users submit products which are listed in a linear format daily. | PG 85, 126

BetaRelease | Platform regularly releasing beta tested tools; allows you to discover useful tools. | PG 85

Steve Blank | Silicon Valley entrepreneur recognized for developing the Customer Development method that launched the Lean Startup movement, a methodology which recognized that startups are not smaller versions of large companies, but require their own set of processes and tools to be successful. | PG 86

Mark Suster | An American entrepreneur and venture capitalist. He is currently managing partner at Upfront Ventures. He is a prominent blogger in the startup venture capital world and a mentor at Techstars. | PG 86

Buzzsumo | An essential tool, BuzzSumo facilitates a much deeper understanding of our social footprint and helps us to develop smarter content strategies. | PG 86, 87, 88

Makesmail | Allows you to import individual and company names, and export email addresses to contact them. | PG 88

Mailshake | Stops the sequence when a reply is detected, handles unsubscribe requests, and ignores auto-responders. Belong to as many teams as you like, and invite others to collaborate on your campaigns. | PG 89

GrowthHackers.com | Helps teams work together to accelerate growth | PG 99

Sean Ellis | CEO and founder of GrowthHackers.com, After igniting growth for Dropbox, Eventbrite, LogMeIn and Lookout—each now worth billions of dollars, Sean coined "growth hacking" as the approach he used. | PG 99, 100

Chrome | A freeware web browser, developed by Google LLC. It was first released on September 2, 2008 for Microsoft Windows, and was later ported to Linux, macOS, iOS and Android. | PG 126

AARRR Funnel | A 5-step funnel diagram design for accommodating Acquisition, Activation, Retention, Revenue and Referral Metrics. The AARRR is a relative start up method created by Dave McClure. | PG 128

500 Startup | An early-stage venture fund and seed accelerator founded in 2010 by Dave McClure and Christine Tsai. | PG 128

LinkedIn Sales Navigator | Makes social selling easy with sales tools that focus on helping you find the right prospects to build trusted relationships. | PG 132

Quuu.co | Allows you to automate social media postings. | PG 134

Buffer.com | Makes it easy for businesses and marketing teams to schedule posts, analyze performance, and manage all accounts in one place. | PG 134

Drift App | A conversational marketing platform. With Drift on your website, you can turn your traffic into qualified meetings using our bots 24 hours a day, 7 days a week. | PG 136

Intercom | A US-based software company that produces a messaging platform which allows businesses to communicate with prospective and existing customers within their app, on their website, through social media, or via email. | PG 136

HubSpot | A developer and marketer of software products for inbound marketing and sales, founded by Brian Halligan and Dharmesh Shah in 2006. | PG 136

Branch.io | A mobile marketing and deep linking platform that supercharges your app growth and seamlessly plugs into your marketing stack. | PG 139

Airbnb | A privately-held global company headquartered in San Francisco that operates an online marketplace and hospitality service which is accessible via its websites and mobile apps. | PG 139, 140, 148

Autopilot | Allows you to capture new leads from your website, app or blog and then nurture them with personalized messages, automate repetitive tasks like educating new subscribers, assigning leads, booking appointments and following up sales leads. | PG 142

PandaDoc | A document automation software as a service with built-in electronic signatures, workflow management, a document builder, and CPQ functionality. | PG 143, 145

Uber | A peer-to-peer ridesharing, taxi cab, food delivery, bicycle-sharing, and transportation network company headquartered in San Francisco, California, with operations in 785 metropolitan areas worldwide. | PG 148

Lyft | An on-demand transportation company based in San Francisco, California. It develops, markets, and operates the Lyft car transportation mobile app. | PG 148

Lime | An electric scooter and bike sharing app whose micro-mobility solutions include dock free rental bikes, e-assist bikes, and electric scooters that are available anytime to get you across town or across campus. | PG 148

Kickofflabs | Allows you to quickly and easily setup refer-a-friend style giveaways, sweepstakes, and product launches. | PG 148

Viral-loops.com | A template-based viral and referral marketing solution for modern marketers. | PG 148

Manychat | A1 bot platform used through Facebook Messenger for marketing, e-commerce, and support. | PG 136

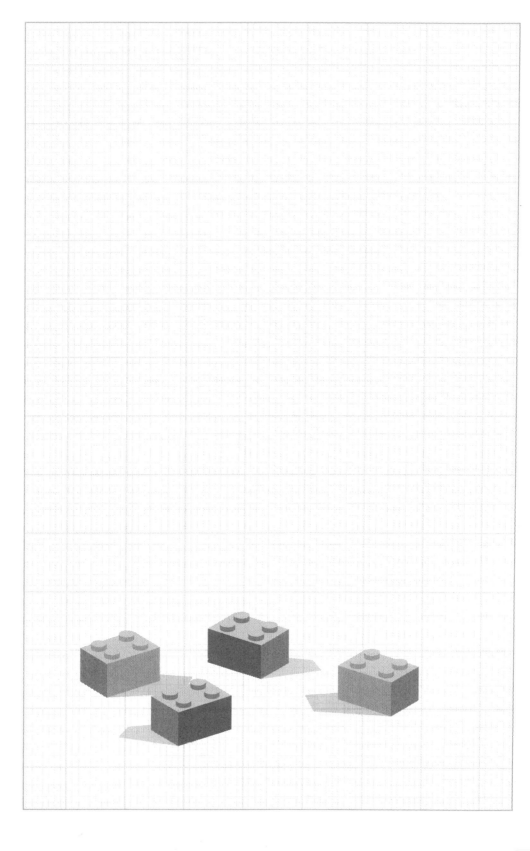

GLOSSARY

OF TERMS + INDEX

KPI's | KEY PERFORMANCE INDICATORS | TOOLS AND ACTIONS USED TO MEASURE AND MONITOR AN ORGANIZATION'S GOAL-ORIENTED PROGRESS. | PG 11, 19

GTM | GO-TO-MARKET STRATEGY | THE METHOD YOU USE TO TAKE YOUR PRODUCT TO MARKET. | PG 11, 12, 19, 38, 39, 45, 88, 91, 124, 150, 151

CREATIVE TRACTION METHODOLOGY | PROVIDES A FRAMEWORK FOR STARTUPS THAT HELPS FOUNDERS GROWTH HACK THEIR PATH TOWARDS TRACTION. | PG 12, 162

GROWTH HACKING | THE MOST AGILE WAY TO RUN SALES AND MARKETING IN THE AGE OF INNOVATION, TO INCREASE THE ODDS OF YOUR BUYER PERSONA TO ENGAGE WITH YOUR PRODUCT. | PG 17, 25, 31, 32, 38

HACKS | A MORE EFFICIENT AND EFFECTIVE WAY OF ACHIEVING A GOAL OR DESIRE THAN IS PUBLICLY ADMINISTERED. | PG 153

POC's | PROOF OF CONCEPTS | A DEMONSTRATION TO VERIFY CERTAIN CONCEPTS OR THEORIES IN PREPARATION FOR REAL-WORLD APPLICATION. | PG 14, 48

PMF | PRODUCT/MARKET FIT | WHEN YOUR PRODUCT SATISFIES MARKET DEMANDS. | PG 38, 44, 45

IP | INTELLECTUAL PROPERTY | A PROCESS, IDEA OR INVENTION DERIVED FROM THE INTELLECT AND RECOGNIZED WITH OWNERSHIP. | PG 39, 149, 151

START BEFORE YOU START | BEGIN STRATEGIZING BEFORE YOUR PRODUCT IS COMPLETE. SO LONG AS YOU HAVE AN ASSUMPTION FOR YOUR TARGET AUDIENCE, YOU CAN BEGIN TO CRAFT YOUR STRATEGY. | PG 75

THE PAINKILLER EXERCISE | HOW YOU CONVEY YOUR PRODUCT AS A PAINKILLER, RATHER THAN A VITAMIN THROUGH THE STRATEGY OF COMMUNICATION. | PG 60, 63-64

RECALIBRATE YOUR MINDSET | RETHINK WHAT YOU KNOW ABOUT SALES AND MARKETING AND HOW TO BRING A PRODUCT TO MARKET. | PG 73

VITAMIN | A NURTURING PRODUCT OR SERVICE THAT DOES NOT CAUSE A PERSONA TO CRAVE THE PRODUCT OR SERVICE THEY ARE ENGAGING WITH. | PG 59

PAINKILLER | A PRODUCT OR SERVICE THAT LEADS THE PERSONA TO CRAVE MORE ENGAGEMENT. | PG 59

EXECUTING COHERENTLY | IMPLEMENTING THE RIGHT TOOLS AND TACTICS AT EACH STAGE OF THE FUNNEL TO ENSURE YOUR PERSONA ENJOYS THEIR ENGAGEMENT WITH YOUR BRAND. | PG 125

INTRAPRENEUR | A MANAGER WORKING WITHIN A COMPANY OR CORPORATION WHO FOCUSES ON INNOVATIVE PRODUCT DEVELOPMENT AND MARKETING. | PG 43, 49, 85

CAC | CUSTOMER ACQUISITION COSTS | THE PRICE YOU PAY TO ACQUIRE—I.E. THE WORTH OF—A NEW CUSTOMER. | PG 44

CAB STRATEGY | CUSTOMER ADVISORY BOARD STRATEGY | APPROACHING CORPORATE EXECUTIVES IN YOUR INDUSTRY BY UTILIZING EMBEDDED STRATEGIC PROMOTION AND CONCISE COMMUNICATION. | PG 46, 48

B2B | BUSINESS TO BUSINESS | REFERS TO SITUATIONS WHERE ONE BUSINESS MAKES A COMMERCIAL TRANSACTION WITH ANOTHER. | PG 46, 98, 131, 136, 142, 167

LOIs | LETTERS OF INTENT | A WAY OF INTRODUCING YOURSELF TO YOUR CUSTOMER BEFORE THEY SEE YOUR PRODUCT. | PG 48, 50

MARKET PENETRATION | A MEASURE OF AN INDIVIDUAL PRODUCT'S SUCCESS AMIDST THE MARKET. | PG 50, 99

VALUE PROPOSITION [VALIDATION] | A SIMPLIFIED REASONING FOR A CUSTOMER TO ENGAGE A SPECIFIC PROCESS. | PG 12,19,55-56, 60-64, 81-82,98,162

USP | UNIQUE SELLING PROPOSITION | A UNIQUE REASONING FOR A PRODUCT OR SERVICE'S SUCCESS. | PG 56, 63

"ME TOO" PRODUCT | A PRODUCT WITHOUT THE NECESSARY TRACTION TO STAND OUT WITHIN A MARKET. | PG 56, 61

TRIGGER-BASED COMMUNICATION | ESSENTIAL FOUNDATIONAL TACTICS FOR GAINING PERSONA ATTENTION. | PG 66

STRATEGIC PROMOTION | THE WAY IN WHICH YOU OFFER WORDS TO YOUR TARGET AUDIENCE. | PG 27, 74, 79, 92, 109, 132, 137, 163

RAPID VALUE ASSESSMENT EXERCISE | AN EXERCISE WHICH ALLOWS YOU TO RAPIDLY ASSESS YOUR VALUE PROPOSITION—I.E. HOW YOU ARE DIFFERENT—SO YOU CAN ANALYZE YOUR COMPETITION AND UNDERSTAND THEIR VALUE PROPOSITION—I.E. HOW THEY CONVEY THEMSELVES. | PG 60, 63

BUSINESS CANVAS STRATEGY | A MORE DETAILED EXERCISE OF ASSESSING YOUR VALUE IN CONTRAST TO COMPETITORS. | PG 60, 61

TRIGGER-BASED MARKETING | PHRASING THINGS IN A WAY THAT TRIGGERS YOUR PERSONA TO TAKE ACTION ON YOUR SERVICE OR PRODUCT UPON OUTREACH. | PG 67, 79

SCARCITY STRATEGY | RATHER THAN SIMPLY OFFERING A PRODUCT, YOU MAKE THE PRODUCT SEEM RARE, SO THAT YOUR TARGET AUDIENCE STARTS TO CRAVE YOUR OFFERING. | PG 67, 68, 79, 83, 96, 137

STRATEGY OF LIMITATION | LIMITING THE AVAILABILITY OF A PRODUCT, SERVICE OR EVENT TO INCREASE DESIRABILITY. | PG 68, 68

LOCATION-BASED TRIGGER | WHERE YOU LIMIT A PRODUCT, SERVICE OR EVENT BY GEO-LOCATION. | PG 68

LEADERBOARD | A LIST OF TOP USERS ON ANY SITE OR APP. | PG 76, 148

I DON'T KNOW STRATEGY | A STRATEGY THAT CAUSES INVESTORS OR THE LIKE TO RESPOND IN A SURPRISED WAY ABOUT WHAT YOU DO. | PG 80

DISCOVER THE UNCLUTTERED CHANNEL | DISCOVER AND APPLY THE UNCLUTTERED CHANNEL—I.E. DISTRIBUTING THE PRODUCT TO MARKET IN A WAY THAT INFLUENCES YOUR TARGET AUDIENCE—BY LEVERAGING NEXT-GEN TOOLS. | PG 84

GIVE BEFORE YOU ASK | WHERE YOU TAKE YOUR AUDIENCE BEYOND WHAT THEY EXPECT TO GET FROM YOUR PRODUCT. | PG 92

VALUE LADDER OFFERING | A LADDER OF DRAFTED STEPS LISTED IN ORDER OF PROJECT COMPLETION PRECEDENCE. ON TOP OF THE LADDER YOU FIND THE ULTIMATE ACHIEVEMENT YOU ARE WORKING TOWARDS IN YOUR ACTIVITY. | PG 94,98

INCLUSIVE MARKETING ACTIVITIES | ACTIVITIES WHERE YOU INCLUDE YOUR TARGET PERSONA, MAKING THEM A PART OF YOUR PRODUCT, RATHER THAN JUST TRYING TO SELL TO THEM. IN OTHER WORDS, MAKING YOUR TARGET AUDIENCE A PART OF WHAT YOU DO; MAKING THEM FEEL LIKE A PART OF YOUR BRAND. | PG 95

ONLINE TO OFFLINE STRATEGY | RATHER THAN APPROACHING YOUR BUYER PERSONA THROUGH A CHANNEL, YOU TAKE THE RELATIONSHIP OFFLINE. | PG 97

LUNCH-AND-LEARN | A COORDINATED MEETING WHERE YOU SHARE AND SWAP SKILLS WHILE ENJOYING A MEAL. | PG 98

MEP | MINIMUM EXPECTED PRODUCT | THE MINIMUM YOU CAN PROVIDE TO USE TO ACQUIRE VALIDATION. | PG 103

STRATEGY OF CONTROLLED PROCRASTINATION | GIVING SPACE AND PROACTIVELY PROCRASTINATING AS A MEANS OF COUNTERINTUITIVELY ACCELERATING THE SALE CYCLE. | PG 106

FOMO | THE FEAR OF MISSING OUT | RATHER THAN MERELY OFFERING YOUR PRODUCT TO EVERY MEMBER OF YOUR TARGET AUDIENCE, LIMITING THE ACCESS AND AVAILABILITY TO HOOK THEIR INTEREST. | PG 109

PRESENTING VALUE + STEPPING AWAY | YOU PRESENT VALUE (EXPLAINING WHAT YOU DO) BY FINISHING THE CONVERSATION WITH A DETACHED APPROACH, RATHER THAN WITH A FIXED CALL TO ACTION. | PG 111

PROACTIVE MEETING COORDINATION | THIS STRATEGY IS A MEANS OF PROACTIVELY HELPING TO ASSURE A CLIENT IN MAKING THE DECISION TO MOVE FORWARD WITH A DEAL. | PG 114

MEETING TO MEETING TO WIN | EVERY TIME YOU CONNECT WITH YOUR POTENTIAL PROSPECT, NEVER END WITHOUT USHERING THEM FROM MEETING, TO MEETING, TO WIN. | PG 117

COHERENT ACTIVITY PLAN | A PLAN OF BREAKING DOWN YOUR PERSONA'S JOURNEY INTO STEPS, TO UNDERSTAND AND ACTIVATE THEIR INTEREST IN YOUR PRODUCT OR SERVICE. | PG 125

THE G-AARRR FUNNEL | AN EMBELLISHED VERSION OF ACCELERATOR 500 STARTUP'S CLASSIC AARRR FUNNEL, WHERE YOU BREAK DOWN THE CUSTOMER JOURNEY, NOW WITH AN ADDED FIRST PHASE TO ACHIEVE FUNNEL SUCCESS. | PG 128

LINKEDIN ACQUISITION STRATEGY | A HACK FOR ACQUIRING CONTACT INFORMATION FOR INVESTOR OR PERSONA OUTREACH. | PG 134, 141

DEEP-LINKING | A MEANS OF SENDING A VISITOR DIRECTLY TO THEIR INTENDED PAGE ON A WEBSITE RATHER THAN TO A LANDING PAGE. | PG 139

CRM | CUSTOMER RELATIONSHIP MANAGEMENT | THE MANAGEMENT OF A COMPANY'S INTERACTION WITH BOTH CURRENT AND POTENTIAL CUSTOMERS. | PG 139

RETARGETING STRATEGY | RETARGETING HELPS YOU TO KEEP YOUR BRAND IN FRONT OF PROSPECTS WHO HAVEN'T YET BECOME CUSTOMERS. | PG 140

STOP SPRAYING AND PRAYING | STOP SPRAYING YOUR EFFORTS, AND PRAYING THAT SOMETHING STICKS. INSTEAD, PLAN YOUR FUNNEL. | PG 125, 127

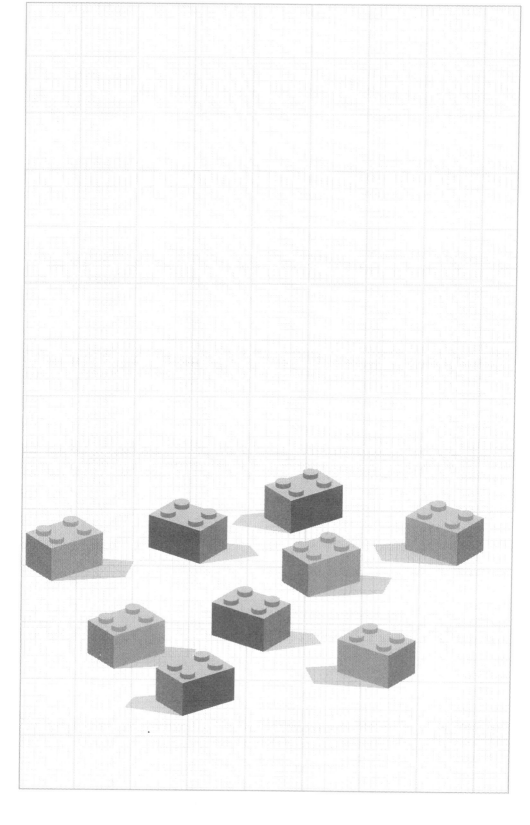

AUTHOR BIO

TOMMASO DI BARTOLO

Serial Entrepreneur and Startup Investor, Author, Advisor and a Faculty at the University of California Berkeley, Tommaso has built four tech startups from scratch, and has two exits under his belt.

Tommaso is passionate about sharing his lessons learned from nearly two decades of entrepreneurial tech expertise as a frequent keynote speaker and advisor to startup accelerators such as Google Launchpad, Draper University, and The Alchemist, and as well serves the roles of faculty member at UC Berkeley and guest lecturer at Stanford University.

Based in Silicon Valley, Tommaso's current 2019 projects include Awesm Ventures, an early stage investment firm that, unlike others, partners with corporations to drive external innovation by leveraging data-driven startups, and The SiliconVal.ly Institute, that provides immersive educational courses and MBAs to corporate executives focusing on digital transformation and corporate innovation, in collaboration with global ivy league universities.

His current mission is to contribute to reducing the failure rate for innovation by helping tech companies gain traction and corporates innovation.

Tommaso is married, and father to two wonderful boys; He isa passionate gourmet foodie who has lived on three continents and speaks six languages.

To follow Tommaso, request access to his closed group called *What It Takes* http://tools.creative-traction.com/RequestGroupAccess and for more information about his next Keynote head to TommasoDiBartolo.com.

Made in the USA
Columbia, SC
06 March 2020